THE DALES OF
YORKSHIRE

THE DALES OF YORKSHIRE

A PORTRAIT

Richard Muir

MACMILLAN LONDON

For Mr George Gill in gratitude for the many times when he has shared his recollections of happier days in the Yorkshire Dales.

My thanks are due to Martin and Rosamund Gaunt and to Bill Mitchell.

Also by Richard Muir

The English Village
Riddles in the British Landscape
The Shell Guide to Reading the Landscape
The Lost Villages of Britain
History from the Air
Visions of the Past (with Christopher Taylor)
The National Trust Guide to Prehistoric and Roman Britain (with
     Humphrey Welfare)
A Traveller's History of Britain and Ireland
The Shell Countryside Book (with Eric Duffey)
The Shell Guide to Reading the Celtic Landscapes
The National Trust Guide to Dark Age and Medieval Britain
The National Trust Guide to Rivers of Britain (with Nina Muir)
Landscape and Nature Photography
Hedgerows (with Nina Muir)
Old Yorkshire
The Countryside Encyclopaedia
Fields (with Nina Muir)
Barleybridge
Portraits of the Past
Castles and Strongholds

Copyright © Richard Muir 1991

First published 1991 by
MACMILLAN LONDON LIMITED
4 Little Essex Street London WC2R 3LF
and Basingstoke

Associated companies in Auckland, Delhi, Dublin, Gaborone, Hamburg, Harare, Hong Kong, Johannesburg, Kuala Lumpur, Lagos, Manzini, Melbourne, Mexico City, Nairobi, New York, Singapore and Tokyo

A CIP catalogue record for this book is available from the British Library.

ISBN 0–333–49786–4

Designed by Behram Kapadia
Typeset by Wearside Tradespools, Fulwell, Sunderland
Printed in Hong Kong

Contents

Introduction

The Yorkshire Dales National Park covers an area of 680 square miles (1765 sq. km) but the real region of the Yorkshire Dales is larger than this; this book deals with the larger natural region rather than the smaller, artificial one. Here I cover the area of the Park and also expanses of characteristic Dales countryside in Nidderdale, Ribblesdale and Lower Wensleydale. This definition excludes areas to the north and west of North Yorkshire but includes a small part of Lancashire in the Forest of Bowland to the south of the county. My division of territory is as intuitive as any other and there can be no hard and fast demarcation since countryside with Dales-like qualities extends north-eastwards into Northumberland and south-westwards into Derbyshire.

Not too much more than a century ago visitors of a hardy disposition began to establish the roots of a tourist industry, but before this time the Dales region was a largely forgotten backwater of upland country. James Herriot encapsulated and broadcast the qualities of the area and its people with a success that the Brontës never achieved. Through most of history the Dalesfolk fought their own fights and expected little from the rest of the country; this expectation was seldom disappointed.

In the seventeenth and eighteenth centuries and for much of the nineteenth the region experienced a strong surge of population growth, if not prosperity, as a result of the expansion of the lead and textiles industries, the latter based on linen and hand-knitting. When these industries withered in later Victorian times nothing arose to take their place. Villages emptied and when they filled again it was not with trueborn Dalesfolk. Meanwhile the hill farmers clung doggedly to their hillside perches, enduring scarcely imaginable degrees of privation rather than leave the view and the only life they knew. This was never a region of riches. After the Norman Conquest the ravaged valleys were carved up between the vast hunting reserves of the kings and aristocrats and the great sheep ranges of the newly founded monasteries. Yet in the end it was the dogged farmers who survived to see the hunting forests and the Cistercian empires

decay and who proceeded to create the landscapes of wall and field barn, meadow, pasture and fell grazing which are the essence of the countryside.

Given the adversity of life in the Dales – the bloody wars with the Scots, the persecution by southerners after the failure of the Pilgrimage of Grace, the poverty of the spinner and weaver, the hardships of the mines and the long cruel winters – the toughness of the Dalesfolk is not surprising. But what in history or the setting can explain the warmth and humour of the people? A stubborn nature, which borders on bloody-mindedness, has allowed the people of the Dales to endure centuries of hardship and yet today they stand by with an apparent meekness as strangers price them out of their villages, and as policies formed in the south threaten their livelihoods. In Wales similar processes have led to clannish isolation and in some cases to arson. Yet in the Dales visitors from the south are still washed by a warm tide of good humour.

As a Dalesman born, if not entirely bred, I write about the region with some passion – not least because I can remember Nidderdale as it was thirty or more years ago, when almost every aspect of life and landscape was better and richer than it is today. Some of the views expressed here and there may seem a little outspoken, but the reader is unlikely to realise how tempered and diluted they really are. For countless childhood hours I wandered up and down the dale with a sheepdog or two in tow. My early love of the countryside was not of an intellectual kind, but gradually I began to wonder about the age of the woods and fields. Almost before I could read I memorised all the pictures in a cherished bird book but it was only later that I began to appreciate that birds had habitats and behaviour and that man was their greatest enemy. In the field where I played there were buttercups, daisies, cowslips, harebells and milkmaids growing. Now it is full of houses.

I would use a jam jar to catch small tortoiseshell, red admiral and grayling butterflies, but we never see the grayling any more. Nor the corncrake nor the sandmartin. Over the years I taught myself how to unravel some of the secrets of the countryside and of how it was made. In this book I attempt to explain the chapters in the creation of the countryside of the Yorkshire Dales, but as the memories flood back it so often feels that I am reviewing a play upon which the curtain is just about to close. The anguish is strong because so much has survived and so much could still be saved.

PART ONE

CHAPTER I

The Natural Setting

Dales are valleys, the word being brought here by Viking settlers a thousand or more years ago. But now most people have forgotten the meaning of 'dale' (*dalr* as it originally was), so that when they speak of the Dales they talk not only of the valleys but also of the fells, the expanses of hill and plateau which lie between them. Most of the major dales take their names from the rivers which they contain – Wharfedale, Nidderdale and Swaledale. However, the dale holding the River Ure is Wensleydale, which derives from the name of what was once a thriving little market town. Only occasionally do you hear the old name of Uredale or Yoredale. Then there is a host of lesser dales – Bishopdale, Coverdale, Langstrothdale and many more, whose names come from varied sources.

The dales have been carved into the rocks of the Pennines by the remorseless erosive action of their rivers. This sculpting of the landscape has continued for millions of years and it will continue until there is not a bank or hillock left to be ground away. The rocks upon which the scenery is engraved, mainly sandstones and limestones, are older still than the rivers. These rocks are a little more ancient than the coal deposits near the industrial towns to the south of our region.

While moving through the Dales on a perfect day it is easy to be beguiled by the beauty of the countryside. On autumn days when northern winds impart crystal-clear air, Swaledale and the tributary valleys of Wharfedale seem perfect fairylands. At times such as these one may set aside all thoughts of questioning and interpreting the scenes and simply bask in their beauty. Sooner or later, however, any enquiring mind will seek the meaning behind the splendour. Why is Nidderdale darker, lusher and more heavily wooded than the open emerald and silver expanses of Wharfedale? And why do we find peaty moors of heather and bracken on some upland plateaux and close-cropped sheep pasture on others?

OPPOSITE ABOVE
Gritstone tors at Brimham Rocks

OPPOSITE BELOW
The lower falls at Aysgarth

There is an old cliché, originating I remember not where, which maintains that 'The answer lies in the soil.' In the case of the scenery of the Dales this is frequently true, for the different soils and the rocks from which they derive are responsible for many of the qualities and contrasts in the unfolding scene. Rocks and soil could happily be left to the geologist, mason and gardener were it not for the fact that they are the very foundations and substances of landscape. Only limestone could endow us with the scenic extravaganzas of potholes and caverns, and only gritstone (or perhaps granite) could weather to produce the weirdly sculpted outcrops of Brimham Rocks. Equally, were the moisture-guzzling limestone not so widespread there would be vast expanses of sodden ground and none of the vistas of pale walls, silvery scars and finely turfed pastures which epitomise the region.

When we enquire about the origins of the rocky building blocks of scenery, we encounter a depth of antiquity which we can scarcely comprehend, for the main rocks are rather more than 300 million years old. Imagine a landscape ground down low by the forces of erosion which basks in sub-tropical sun. We have travelled back beyond the age of man or mammals and birds, back too beyond the age of dinosaurs, and fishes are the most advanced lifeforms on earth. The sea begins to invade across the sagging plain. Its waters are vibrant with life; tiny organisms live briefly before dying, their shells and skeletons fluttering slowly to the sea floor. Little changes for millions of years but meanwhile a chalky mud composed of limy shell debris accumulates on the sea floor in a thickness great enough to engulf the tallest skyscraper. It is from this chalky sludge that the silver limestone has evolved.

Then the balance of nature begins to change. To the north of our sea lies a mountainous mass of land, and the rivers flowing seawards from these mountains become torrents charged with coarse particles of grit washed down from the eroding uplands. This sand is washed out across the white sludge of the sea bed and accumulates in great depths, the sea floor being borne downwards by the weight of the sediments. Eventually the rocks which have formed on the sea floor emerge into the light, the gritstone known as Millstone Grit forming a tough blanket above the limestone.

Now much of this blanket has been worn completely away to expose the limestone beneath. The gritstone survives in places. It provides a hard, slab-like capping to the 'mountains' of Ingleborough and Pen-y-ghent. In Nidderdale it appears again, along with bands of coal, sandstone and shale. During the period between the laying down of the limestone and the accumulating of grits the conditions in and around our ancient sea fluctuated. Sometimes mud was deposited, sometimes sand or limestone; and sometimes forests, destined to become coal, flourished beside lagoons. As a result banded rocks of rapidly alternating beds of shale, sandstone and limestone were formed. These 'Yoredale' rocks can often be recognised as they outcrop on hillsides, for their different components weather at different rates to produce a staircase-like effect. The alternation of rocks of different types across a river bed can also produce sequences of rapids and waterfalls – no valley in Britain can rival Wensleydale in this respect.

When the rocks of the region, now hard and compacted, arose from the sea, rivers began to form and to commence their work of erosion. Meanwhile, great tensions in the earth's crust were released by faulting, which raised or lowered blocks of countryside; this, together with folding, which twisted and crumpled the layers of rock, created a broken, hilly landscape. Most of the rivers, like the Aire, Wharfe, Nidd, Ure and Swale, adjusted their courses to the gentle eastward slope towards the North Sea, were gathered together in the Ouse and merged in the Humber. The Dee and the Ribble adopted a westward course, flowing briefly and swiftly to the plains of Lancashire and the Irish Sea. As the rivers collected rainwater or snowmelt from their catchments and drained the countryside, so particles of grit were swept along and, in times of flood, stones and boulders were rolled along the river beds. The friction and grinding accomplished by the contents of the waters gradually engraved the valleys deeper and deeper into the landscape. Now they exist as easy corridors for movement so that most visitors explore the length of a chosen dale rather than journeying across the grain of the country. The trip from one dale to the next usually involves a steep climb by a narrow snaking road until the flatter ground of a broad plateau is reached, and then a sharp and winding descent into the valley beyond.

No visit to the Dales is complete without an exploration of at least one of the magnificent 'forces' or waterfalls – and no other region of Britain can boast such a spectacular collection of falls and rapids. They are the creations of geological history and are particularly numerous in Wensley-dale, where the swift alternation of hard and soft bands in the Yoredales strata favours the formation of broken river courses. The most frequently visited of these falls is probably Aysgarth Falls, near the village of this name. Confined here by the steep flanks of the valley, the Ure crosses a series of terraces which extend along the valley for more than a mile. In summer the waters spill gently down the steps in the geological staircase, but during the winter floods the stepped profile of the river bed vanishes beneath a roaring torrent of foam. Here the falls are more than the creation of differences in rock type for the severe glacial erosion of Bishopdale, which joins the Ure a little way downstream, produced a steep drop in the bed, which is gradually being worn back upstream by river erosion.

Quite different in appearance is Hardraw Force, near Hawes, which is reached via the Green Dragon pub. Here a stream, or 'beck', plunges vertically into the glacial trough of Wensleydale for a distance of 90 feet

(27 m). Since the end of the Ice Age the force has been worn back upstream for a distance of more than 200 yards (c. 185 m), a particularly potent and rapid example of the way that falls invariably migrate upstream until they eventually merge into a smoothly graded channel. The lip of the waterfall is formed of tough limestone, below this is sandstone and then soft shale. The swirling, toppling waters have undercut the softer rocks so that it is possible to walk right behind the white veil of the falls. The cliff amphitheatre surrounding the falls creates a spectacular setting – one which has been used for staging brass-band concerts.

Thornton Force is the climax of a sequence of rapids and cascades near Ingleton, where a beck tumbles steeply to resume its ancient course after being diverted by a dumped mass of glacial debris. Again, a tough lip of limestone crowns the weaker rocks of the face of the fall, which in this case are slates. Lower down in the Ingleton glens the becks tumble across very old slates and a tough gritstone known as 'greywacke', making the locality a mecca for geologists.

In Swaledale the village of Keld is bracketed by falls: Wain Wath Force, Kisdon Force on the Swale with East Gill Falls nearby where a beck makes its stormy approach to the river. Falls can be found in or beside villages like Gayle, Hawes or West Burton, while the clear pools at the foot of falls like Janet's Foss near Malham were once used for sheep-washing. In the Yorkshire Dales the falls and rapids are too numerous for all to be mentioned. Some, such as Mill Gill Force above Askrigg, are celebrated and others, like Scaleber Force by the Settle–Kirkby Malham road, though spectacular are little visited. In addition there are a few man-made falls which are legacies of the days of water-powered industry. A most notable example is the broad staircase at Birstwith in Nidderdale.

Waterfalls developed rapidly when they were eroded by torrents of meltwater released at the end of the Ice Ages. Glaciation had many other important effects on the landscape of the Dales. As the climate chilled at the start of each of the four great Ice Ages the high western face of the Pennines intercepted the snow-bearing clouds. With each passing year less and less of the snow on the Pennines melted until eventually even the high plateaux vanished beneath the blanket of ice. Only the loftiest of the summits rose above the dead, white landscape where the arctic winds drove the snow flurries across the ice sheets, glaciers and crevasses. The last Ice Age lasted from about 70,000 to around 12,000 years ago and was particularly severe. Two ice caps formed in the great snow-gathering grounds around the high western face of the Pennines, expanded across the high plateaux and sent glacial fingers down the valleys. Where the old river gradients were steep the glacial erosion was potent, but when the glaciers reached the plains of the Vale of York the momentum for erosion was lost. In addition to the home-grown ice sheets, others expanded into the Dales

from Scotland, Ireland and the Cheviots. Transported glacial boulders known as 'erratics' were carried into the region from Scotland and the Lake District and dumped by melting ice at heights of up to 1935 feet (590 m). Here they can still be found as monuments to the not-so-distant times when the Dales resembled modern Greenland. Blocks of greywacke gritstone the size of small motorcars were plucked from the floor of Crummack Dale and carried southwards, then dumped on the limestone surface on the southern slopes of Ingleborough. Here they stand stranded, recalling the time when the glacier in Ribblesdale ploughed southwards across dale and fell.

The erosive power of the glaciers, which used their loads of rocks and gravel to scour the countryside like sandpaper, could be immense. Upper Wharfedale and Bishopdale were heavily glaciated and display the classic 'U'-shaped glacial cross-section, as though a great gouge has been thrust along the valleys. Ice accumulating on Langstrothdale Chase was diverted into two streams by the great bulk of Buckden Pike and was then channelled into the valleys. The same hill shielded the neighbouring valley of Walden, so that here we can gain an impression of the form of valleys before glaciation. It is shallower with a 'V'-shaped cross-section. Rugged cliffs known as 'scars' are seen flanking most valleys in limestone country and these scars exist where the valley glaciers stripped away the old accumulations of soil and weathered rock to expose the bare rock faces.

Rock debris worn and prised from the uplands and valleys was often ground as fine as flour and then plastered on the slopes and plains. Many of the valleys on the Howgill Fells are choked with this glacial debris or 'till'. In some places decaying ice, which was heavily burdened with till, was moulded by the retreating ice to form flocks of smooth, blister-shaped hills known as 'drumlins'. Drumlin fields can be seen in the upper valleys of the Ure and Ribble and between the Ribble and the Aire to the south of Settle. In Wensleydale drumlins are amalgamated into elongated lobes of till which have diverted the tributary valleys eastwards. Hardraw Force and Mill Gill Force are waterfalls which formed as their becks were diverted to flow around these 'drift tails'.

The warming of the climate and the wasting of the ice unleashed thundering rivers of meltwater. Such meltwater was largely responsible for the creation of Gordale Scar, near Malham, perhaps the most imposing feature in the landscape of the Dales. The gorge, with its towering walls which seem to clasp the visitor in the pit of a great geological vice, was gouged along a line of weakness in the limestone by plummeting flood-waters, although today it houses only a modest stream. In the dark depths of the gorge it bursts from the cliff in a beautiful cascade to produce one of the finest scenic cameos one may ever hope to witness. Not far away on the other side of the village is Malham Cove, a 230-foot (70-m) high limestone cliff. This was carved by a glacier and then shaped by hurtling meltwater, at which time the cove will have existed as an awe-inspiring waterfall. Now hardly any water from Malham Tarn remains above ground long enough to fall down the rock face; some re-emerges at the foot of the cove, where there is a flooded cavern, while some re-emerges downstream of the village.

As the last Ice Age reached its close the Dales region was awash with torrents of meltwater and plastered with bare expanses of till and water-borne sand. Myriad wild flowers which are seen today in the sub-Arctic tundra regions will have briefly coloured the barren scene. At this time lakes were numerous in the sodden countryside, but gradually the dams of ice-dumped 'moraine' were breached and river sediments filled the lake floors. Today the region is rather impoverished in lakes though two examples do attract visitors: Malham Tarn only survives in its setting of porous limestone because it rests on an ice-scooped basin of ancient slate, its stream dammed by glacial debris. Lovely Semer Water is the remnant of a once much larger lake which formed from meltwater ponded back by a glacial moraine. Gradually it is shrinking as streams unload their burdens of silt on the lake floor.

Were limestone not so widespread in the Yorkshire Dales then lakes would doubtless be more numerous. Limestone, however, is a thirsty rock honeycombed with fissures enlarged by rainfall, which becomes a mild form of carbonic acid as it falls through the atmosphere. In Ice Age times the limestone behaved like any other rock, for the fissures and crevices were sealed by ice. However, when the ice melted streams were able to sink and burrow and to create the finest subterranean landscapes of potholes and caverns in Britain.

Distinctive landscapes were also formed upon the land surface. The ice and torrents of meltwater scoured and washed away the life-supporting soil cover on the upland levels. The networks of fissures were enlarged by trickling rainwater, so that when more rain fell it was able to find a way underground, carrying with it any soil particles which had begun to develop upon the barren surface. The result was the formation of expanses of bare white stone known as 'limestone pavements'. The pavements consist of fairly flat-topped blocks called 'clints', which are separated by deeply incised fissures or 'grikes'. Walking across limestone pavement in the dark or after snow is a hazardous venture, for the terrain might have been created to induce sprained ankles. The most frequently visited pavement is the one standing above the great cliff of Malham Cove but there are other and grander examples, like Southerscales Scars on the north-western flanks of Ingleborough.

Often becks and trickles slip furtively into their underground courses, but sometimes their departure is more spectacular and a yawning pothole has formed at the junction of light and darkness. The best-known example is Gaping Gill on the eastern slopes of Ingleborough, which can be reached via a pleasant walk from Clapham. Here the Fell Beck takes the most dramatic departure imaginable, falling vertically for a distance of 340 feet (103 m) and then entering a subterranean chamber large enough to house a cathedral. Other notable potholes include Hull Pot and Hunt Pot on the western side of Pen-y-ghent and Alum Pot on the northern side of Ingleborough. More accessible to the motorist is the group of potholes known as the Buttertubs on the high pass between Swaledale and Wensleydale. Here, streams seeping from a bog on Great Shunner Fell tumble into the potholes and follow a short underground course before emerging from a cave about 300 feet (90 m) further down the slope.

Beneath the land surface forgotten rivers and acidic groundwater have created fascinating scenery unknown and unglimpsed before miners and potholers began to explore the cavern labyrinths. There are great tunnels through which rivers hurtle and other tunnels which lie silent and abandoned by their rivers; there are lakes, shafts and gorges. As water percolates through the limestone some of the calcium carbonate is taken into solution and as water drips from the roof of a cavern and splatters on the cavern floor minute traces of lime may be deposited. Over thousands of years these traces form stalactites like needles or veils hanging down from the roof, or stalagmites rising up from the floor. Most of these spectacular formations lie undiscovered or else are accessible only to skilled potholers.

ABOVE *The Wharfedale glaciers undercut the great cliff of Kilnsey Crag*

RIGHT *The glacial lake of Semer Water*

BELOW *One of the potholes on the Buttertubs Pass*

But there are show caves, like Stump Cross Caverns on the Pateley Bridge to Grassington road, and the Ingleborough Cave, where visitors can explore sections of cave systems in safety.

The Stump Cross caves have produced evidence of ancient wildlife in the Dales. Numerous reindeer bones have been found here, perhaps relics of a group of animals washed into a gaping shaft by a flood of meltwater. More unusual are the bones of a fierce predator and scavenger, the wolverine. This animal, today associated with sub-Arctic regions, may have lived here 50,000 or more years ago, before the glaciers plastered boulder clay across the access to the cave system. The rediscovery of the cavern network is believed to have occurred in Victorian times. Lead-miners were attempting to re-establish contact with a vein of lead and when their shaft had been sunk to a depth of more than 40 feet (12 m) they discovered a natural passageway. While the men took lunch a couple of small boys wriggled along the tunnel and returned with stories of the calcite formations they had found.

Plainly the limestone of the Yorkshire Dales provides us with more interest and wonder than can ever be experienced in the course of a single rambling holiday. The gritstone also has much to offer. There are imposing outcrops like the Cow and Calf rocks overlooking Ilkley and the weirdly sculpted pillars and tors at Brimham Rocks, between Ripon and Pateley Bridge. There are also the various remarkable features described later in this book, like the Strid in Wharfedale or How Stean Gorge in Nidderdale. For any visitor who is the least bit responsive to the natural landscape the question is never what to see next, but which.

PART TWO

CHAPTER 2

Roots of the Dalesfolk

No human eyes viewed the Dales when hundreds or thousands of feet of ice filled the valleys and the dark summits stood like islands in a frozen sea. This was a dead and sterile landscape. However, it is possible that drifting bands of hunters penetrated the region during the long mild spells which separated the four great ages of ice. Such groups certainly reached as far north as the Worksop area and traces of their occupation have been found in caves at Creswell Crags. No evidence has been found to prove they reached the Dales but small migrant hunting groups leave little behind.

As the ice decayed and torrents of meltwater washed across the emerging countryside the scene will have seemed almost as barren as that of the glacial era. Many places were stripped of soil while in others belts of ice-dumped debris and swathes of waterborne sand blanketed the land. Slopes slithered and slumped as the thawed ground slipped upon the ice-bound ground beneath and lakes rose and then fell as the exiting waters carved out escape channels. However, uninviting as the scene may have seemed, life soon returned with plants and animals expanding northwards from their glacial refuges, many of which lay in southern Europe. At first the climate was chilly and the habitats fragile, so that the life forms which advanced up the valleys and fells were those adapted for survival in tundra environments such as those of modern Alaska or northern Siberia. They included lichens, like reindeer moss, alpine plants which flowered in the brief mildness of summer and dwarfed and hardy forms of trees like the birch and willow. As the ice retreated from the North Sea salmon could return to the rivers of the Dales and herds of reindeer pushed their migration trails further and further north.

Towed along by drifting herds were predators and scavengers – wolves, foxes and man. The limestone ensured a plentiful supply of habitable caves, but these caves existed as an optional extra to life in the Dales. They were

The Victoria Cave was home to some of the first Dalesmen and women

not a prerequisite of hunting life, for the roaming bands could survive perfectly well in hide tents or other fabricated shelters. However, it is from the floor deposits of these caves that the best evidence of early life has been recovered.

The best known of the cave dwellings sites is the Victoria Cave above and to the east of Settle. It can be reached by a walk long enough to be exhilarating rather than exhausting, and from the plateau just above the cave there are good views of Ingleborough and Pen-y-ghent. Victoria Cave was probably visited by hunting groups around 10,000 years ago but when the cave sediments were excavated traces of far older tenants of the landscape were revealed: the bones of mammoth and also of rhinoceroses and hippopotamuses which plodded and wallowed in the Dales long ago during the warmer interglacial eras. The excavation also produced a bone harpoon while other evidence of visits by ancient man has come from Attermire Cave, also in the vicinity of Settle, Calf Hole Cave near

Grassington, and Dowkerbottom Cave in Wharfedale where, in a later prehistoric period, a grave was hacked into stalagmite, revealing a concern with the afterlife. On Rombalds Moor, between Wharfedale and Airedale, one may still discover chips of flint derived from the tool-making industries of hunters who may well have kindled fires at the mouths of these caves in the course of their hunting forays.

Yorkshire folk are said to be set in their ways and this trait may be deeply rooted, for an interest in caves was maintained long after the apparent advantages had gone. Several caves in the Dales have produced Roman relics and this is strange since the Dalesfolk of those times had many more convenient places in which to live.

For a long time the climate in the Dales was cold and unstable. Around 11,000 BC it began to warm quite rapidly but then there was a swift and savage reversal to near glacial conditions. This trend in turn was reversed, so that by about 8000 BC the climate had become a little warmer than that of today and conditions were ideal for the colonisation of the countryside by broadleafed forest. For the ancient Dalesfolk, however, the changes posed a challenge and lifestyles that were finely tuned to the pursuit of deer and horses across the open, windy plains had to be adapted to the dimness of the encroaching forest.

None of this natural woodland remains but the trees that we see growing today do provide some hints of its composition. Hazel, birch, ash, oak and yew grew on the limestone uplands, while in the moister valleys a woodland of oak, elm and lime developed with alder fringing the rivers and marshes.

Life during this 'Mesolithic' or Middle Stone Age period was migratory, with communities fragmenting and coalescing according to the dictates of the season. Winter will usually have found the members of a hunting clan living together in flimsy huts and shelters beside a river or lake where fish and wildfowl could be taken. After the lean days of spring the hunters will have ascended through the woods to hunt for birds and mammals in the more open upland country, where traces of their temporary campsites are often revealed by the debris from their flint-shaping work. In autumn the families will have been at work in the woods, gathering nuts, shoots and berries and collecting stores of hazelnuts which could be eaten during the short, hungry days of winter. Survival depended upon an intimate know-ledge of the lives and habits of animals and plants so that each resource could be exploited as it became available.

The woods offered all manner of edible roots, shoots, fruits and fungi, but the tree cover made the pursuit of game more difficult. The present landscape of the Dales is one largely shaped by man and the first stage in the creation of a man-made setting began when hunters deliberately removed woodland to provide open grazing and hunting ranges. In some parts of the uplands these operations prevented a natural woodland cover from ever being established, while around 8000 years ago the climate became significantly warmer and wetter than it is today. Forest clearances by man and the natural waterlogging of the soil made conditions on the high gritstone plateaux hostile to woodland. As the trees disappeared so a blanket of acid peat began to accumulate and this then supported communities of plants including heather and cotton grass which were better equipped to tolerate the moist, sour conditions. Drainage was much less of a problem on the limestone areas but it was during the Mesolithic period that the landscape acquired the mauve and amber tones of the heather and bracken moor and the white confetti-like stipple of the cotton-grass bog.

The next great change to affect the countryside of the Dales was entirely wrought by mankind: the introduction of farming. Were we able to survey the landscape as it existed on the eve of the first agricultural revolution we would see scenes very different from those of today. The heather moors on the gritstone surfaces would have a fairly familiar look, though they would be home to many more types of bird than grouse. Broken in places by man-made clearings, the wildwood would cover most of the areas which today we see as green pastures, meadows and field walls. There were no roads, only the tracks trodden by red deer, bears, wolves and other predators. In the skies above, eagles, osprey, kites and buzzards would whirl and soar. The rivers would be undisciplined by dams or embankments and ever liable to flood and wander across the flat valley floors. Lakes born after the glacial era would still be numerous and while the rivers gradually filled them with silt and alders encroached upon their shrinking margins, beaver would be at work making new lakes of their own. So many of the features which epitomise the Dales landscape as we perceive it would be still unborn or masked by the woodland. Even so, touched only lightly by man and home to a broad spectrum of vanished wildlife, the Dales of 7000 years ago must have been a place of enchantment.

It was around 5000 BC that farming was introduced to Britain and it spread quite rapidly across the more fertile lowlands. The region of the Dales was rather peripheral to the main arenas of farming life and for many years the impact of the new way of life was much less than in the plains to the east. The woods, broken in places by clearings, still clothed the slopes to heights of around 1200 feet (366 m) and hunting, fishing and gathering remained the mainstays of life. As farming developed in the Vale of York it is likely that herds from the plains were driven into the Dales to exploit the high summer grazings of the uplands. At such times some of the herdsmen may have ventured further, into Cumbria, where a series of stone-axe 'factories' operated in the Langdales. Some organised trade system operated, for numerous examples of Langdales axes have been found in the region.

In several parts of Britain the New Stone Age and early Bronze Age are associated with spectacular monuments, but in the Dales the endowment is

quite modest. There was no great religious focus here, though one did lie on
the fringes of the region quite close to the Ure at Thornborough near West
Tanfield. Here three gigantic earth and boulder rings were built with banks
10 feet (3 m) high surrounded by ditches 10 feet deep. The nature of the
ceremonies associated with these 'henges' is not known, though in their day
the monuments must have been quite eyecatching, their banks being
garnished with glittering white crystals of gypsum. Another great monument on the eastern margins of the Dales is the Devil's Arrows, three great
pillars of gritstone standing on the edge of Boroughbridge. The Arrows
probably date from the Bronze Age and the stones are likely to have been
hauled here from a grit outcrop at Knaresborough, some six miles (9.5 km)
away.

Within the region the resources of manpower and the concentration of
worshippers were probably too small to allow such great works to be
contemplated. However, there are few monuments so charming as the
stone ring at Yockenthwaite in Langstrothdale. Standing beside the
flickering waters of the upper Wharfe and overlooked by the slopes of Horse
Head Moor and Yockenthwaite Moor, the stones are generally described as
a stone circle, though they are more likely to represent a kerb of boulders
erected around a small tomb.

Castle Dykes henge on the fell between Bishopdale and Wensleydale is a
rustic cousin of the great henges at Thornborough, a round earthbank
around 200 feet (60 m) in diameter with the central sacred 'stage' defined by
an inner ditch. Few ancient burial places have been found within the
region, the most notable example being Giant's Grave near the source of
Pen-y-ghent Gill. It has features in common with other great 'megalithic'
tombs with its stone-walled burial chambers being covered by a huge mound
of earth and rubble. Unfortunately the state of preservation is much poorer
than that of the more famous British examples elsewhere.

During the formative centuries of farming conservative values seem to
have prevailed in the Dales and the assault upon the wildwood was not

dramatic or sustained. Crops of wheat and barley were grown in clearings on the more sheltered and drier sites. New clearings were made, but often these were cropped for a while and then reclaimed by the woodland. Already, however, the region's identity as an area of livestock rather than of cereal farming was established. It would be fascinating to know how many of our farming practices are rooted in the pioneering experiences of 6000 years ago – did the shepherds run specially trained sheepdogs or did the cowmen cut hay and spread the manure from the byres across buttercup pastures? It is all too easy to let sentiment cloud our visions of the past yet difficult to resist the feeling that pioneering farming life here had a richness that we can scarcely imagine.

During the Bronze Age the frontiers of farming were expanded. In other more prosperous and populous parts of Britain there was labour to spare, allowing the leaders of society to indulge in spectacular tomb- and temple-building operations. In the Dales, however, the emphasis remained upon the day-to-day concerns of winning a livelihood from the land.

Two of the Devil's Arrows standing stones

Enigmatical relics of more mystical concerns are represented by gritstone boulders into which are carved cup and cup-and-ring symbols. Such stones can be found on Rombalds Moor, on Snowden Moor above the Washburn Valley and on Ilkley Moor. The best-known example is the Swastika stone just a couple of miles west of Ilkley town centre, by Hebers Ghyll. It is not known whether these carvings were accomplished in the Bronze Age or in the preceding era. The significance of the markings is no less mysterious. All manner of explanations have been proposed – for example, that the symbols were prospectors' marks or intended to collect little pools of rain and be thus associated with a water ritual – but none of the various suggestions seems particularly convincing.

The pattern of living and farming may have varied according to the climate. In the earlier part of the second millennium BC the warm and dry weather seems to have encouraged a drift from the parched limestone to the damper gritstone areas, while a distinct shift to wet conditions in the later part caused a retreat from the moors where peat and bog were expanding. On the plateaux, slopes and valleys clearances became permanent and networks of fields were established. Almost invariably the traces of these fields were obliterated by later developments in farming but they have been recognised in Swaledale near Reeth. On the fells flocks of sheep and herds of cattle will have roamed, and it is quite likely that the areas between the valleys existed as commons even in the Bronze Age. On the lower, better ground there were probably enclosed fields where grain and flax were rotated with pastures while hay meadows in the valley bottoms may have yielded crops of winter fodder.

Although many accounts have little to say about the prehistoric contributions it is more than likely that by the close of the Bronze Age a substantial proportion of the ancestors of present-day Dalesfolk were established in the region. Where the ancestors of these ancestors had come from must remain a mystery. Some will have followed the reindeer here as the last Ice Age withered away. Others may have landed on the east coast and followed the river network into the Dales through the expanding forest, while others still may have arrived driving their herds and flocks, seeking new summer grazings and bringing with them the dawn of farming. We do not know what language these ancient shepherds, ploughmen and cowherds spoke or whether any of their words are still preserved in the place-names of the Dales. But we can be sure that by the start of the Iron Age, around 650 BC, the landscape of the Dales had long since ceased to be a wilderness. The wildwood was greatly reduced and in many places confined to woods of ash, yew and hazel clinging to the valley slopes which were too steep to be tilled or grazed. Nature's world had been replaced by fieldscape and common and the foundations of the modern countryside were well established.

In most parts of Britain the Iron Age was a time of tension and trouble. The farming successes had underwritten a great growth in population but increasing pressure on resources and a shortage of new lands to colonise led to intense rivalries between neighbouring communities. Once more the Yorkshire Dales emerged as a relatively tranquil backwater. While hillforts multiplied in many other parts of Britain few were built in the Dales, notwithstanding the fact that the rolling upland terrain was ideal for such communal fortresses. Nevertheless, if the quantity was low the quality was not, for the Dales contains both the highest and the largest hillforts in Britain.

The 2372-foot (723-m) summit of Ingleborough is ringed by the rampart wall of England's most lofty hillfort. The defended area is pear-shaped and about 15 acres (6 ha) in extent. It is difficult to imagine that people could have lived in such a majestic yet desolate setting and have been prepared to undertake what, for most visitors, is an exhausting ascent as a part of their daily lives. Nonetheless the circular footings of stone huts can be recognised, showing that there were times when the hillfort housed a community and was more than a temporary bolt-hole. The wall was built of Millstone Grit some 13 feet (4 m) thick with the interior of the wall divided by slabs into compartments which were filled with rubble. Sadly, this wall is constantly being pillaged by visitors who apparently regard one of Yorkshire's finest monuments as a convenient quarry for stones to heap on the summit cairn.

The fort at Stanwick, near Richmond, is quite different. This is by far the most extensive hillfort in Britain but because it occupies a lowland site and has fields and roads superimposed upon it there is no impression of grandeur. The visitor can see great banks and ditches, including an excavated and exposed section of rampart, but from the ground it is impossible to comprehend the pattern of the earthworks. The nucleus of the fort is an oval enclosure known as the Tofts, which may have been held by the native British a few years after the Roman landing. This was quite a formidable strongpoint with ramparts towering some 24 feet (7 m) above the surrounding ditch.

The addition of an extension of 124 acres (50 ha) and then one of 593 acres (240 ha) produced the great complex of fortifications, which includes ramparts faced in drystone walling that were 40 feet (12 m) wide and 10 feet (3 m) high and ditches 40 feet (12 m) and 13 feet (4 m) deep.

The two great hillforts in the Dales are linked in speculation and perhaps in fact. After the Roman invasion of Britain, Cartimandua, the Queen of the tribal federation of the Brigantes which dominated the north, accepted a role as a client ruler of the Roman Empire. She then divorced her husband, Venutius, in AD 69 and cohabited with his armour-bearer. At this time Stanwick appears to have existed as a local capital and trading centre.

OPPOSITE ABOVE
Part of the rampart of Bank Slack hillfort with a much more recent wall in the fronting ditch

RIGHT
A boulder on Weston Moor near Ilkley carved with the mysterious cup-and-ring symbols

OPPOSITE BELOW
The 'stone circle' at Yockenthwaite

Venutius launched a tribal revolt against the empire and extended the Stanwick fortifications. Meanwhile the Romans established a legionary fortress at York. It is uncertain whether the Romans clashed with Venutius and the Brigantes at Stanwick or whether the fort was evacuated as the legions advanced. Certainly it would have been difficult to defend the over-extended perimeter of Stanwick against a Roman military machine which was well versed in the techniques of cracking a hillfort. There is a strong possibility, however, that the tribal warriors who abandoned Stanwick withdrew to the windswept summit of Ingleborough, there to vanish into the mists of the Celtic twilight.

A few smaller hillforts existed in the Dales. They include Maiden Castle to the north-west of Reeth. Though a dwarf in comparison to its great Dorset namesake the circular enclosure is defended by a rampart which stands 16 feet (5 m) above its encircling ditch. Bank Slack, at Fewston near

Harrogate, is a promontory protected by double ramparts and there is a very small stone-walled fort in Grass Wood near Grassington.

In the Dales probably more than in most parts of Britain, Iron Age life did not focus on war but on farming. Some grain was grown in the region, as evidenced by the numerous discoveries of gritstone 'querns', pairs of stones between which the grain was milled. Oats, rye and perhaps wheat were cultivated but the emphasis was on pastoral farming. Of bones unearthed at Stanwick those of cattle were most numerous, followed by those of sheep (or goats), pigs and horses. Only about 1 per cent of the bones were of deer or hare, showing that hunting no longer made an important contribution to the diet.

The territory of the Iron Age Brigantes was the largest in Britain, though not the richest or most progressive. The north was a conservative land and whatever part Celtic settlement may have played in moulding the character of some other territories, Bronze Age influences remained powerful in Brigantia. The federation extended from southern Scotland southwards to the Trent, with the old East Riding of Yorkshire being held by the subordinate tribe of the Parisii. The geographer Ptolemy mentioned the existence of nine Brigantian towns, of which two cannot now be linked to any known sites. These were not towns as we understand towns to be but focal points including forts such as Ingleborough and political centres such as Stanwick. Iron Age Dalesfolk would have felt utterly bewildered in even the most modest of towns, for they were people of the farmstead and hamlet.

And so it is quite appropriate that the most visible monuments to Iron Age life take the form of fossilised field patterns. The region contains some of the country's most notable relict fieldscapes. The most frequently viewed is the pattern of field banks or 'lynchets' running down to the beck which issues from the foot of Malham Cove. The most extensive network, probably the finest in Britain, covers the slopes above Grassington. Here, when the sun is low, slanting shadows and tumbled walls still chart the outlines of rural life as it existed 2000 or more years ago: the little irregular fields, the droves where the cowherds walked and the circular traces of ancient homesteads. Other traces of Iron Age fields and dwellings can be found overlooking Wensleydale on the hills of Addlebrough and Pen Hill. In some places the Iron Age fields traverse what has become barren limestone pavement and it is plain that the quality of the land has deteriorated since ancient times. Changes in both climate and farming practice may have had parts to play. Over the greater parts of the Dales the relics of Iron Age farming have been obliterated by later activities so it is not the case that the ancient Dalesfolk only farmed in areas which were desolate. But they did succeed in supporting vigorous little communities in places where only ramblers and sheep now flourish.

CHAPTER 3

Romans, Celts, Saxons and Vikings

W hen the Romans decided to conquer Britain they knew little if anything about the Dales. A triumph was needed to bolster the reputation of the feeble Emperor, Claudius, the English lowlands were rich grainlands and the southern tribes were stirring up dissent among their Celtic cousins in the empire across the water. Having launched a successful invasion of the lowlands in AD 43 the Romans were in no great hurry to discover the Dales. Cartimandua continued to rule but as a client of the empire and what the Brigantes knew of Roman rule they learned second hand. It was the turbulent events of AD 69 (see p. 29) which encouraged the Romans to play a more direct part in northern affairs. In AD 71 they occupied the lowlands of Yorkshire and in the course of the rest of the decade they pacified the Dales.

At this time few if any of the British will have had any realistic perception of the extent and nature of Britain, and many Dalesfolk were probably not aware that they lived on an island. The Romans, in contrast, were blessed with the ability to take a broad view. They could evaluate each component of the territory and assign it a role. As soon as the legions entered the Dales two facts will have become apparent: firstly, the rugged terrain favoured revolt and guerrilla warfare, and secondly, there were no agricultural or industrial fortunes to be made here. Consequently there was no attempt to civilise and develop the region and, like other upland and mountainous areas, it became a military zone patrolled and pacified by the troops but otherwise largely untouched.

The region had a considerable strategic significance, however. It threatened both the fertile and developing regions spread out around the great fortress at York, and it was also home to tribesmen of dubious loyalty

The Roman Cam High Road heading towards the fortress at Bainbridge

who might at any time advance and cut the communication lines needed to support legions holding the northern frontier or engaging in the periodic attempts to conquer Scotland. The policing of the area was essential. But the news was not all negative. The imperial market and legionary quartermasters will have welcomed the wool, hides and meat produced in the Dales and there was also another significant resource – lead – which was needed for plumbing, waterproofing and various other uses. Mines, which may already have been opened, were exploited at Greenhow, above Pateley Bridge and in Arkengarthdale. Most probably they were worked by Brigantian slaves who had offended their colonial masters in one way or another. Later mining operations have obliterated the traces of Roman activity although two pigs of lead cast in AD 81 and bearing an imperial inscription on one side and the abbreviation 'Brig' for Brigantia on the other were discovered on Hayshaw Moor in 1731. Other pigs have been found dating to the reigns of Trajan (AD 98–117) and Hadrian (AD 117–38).

The invading legions advanced through the Dales to the Slainmore Pass and thence to Carlisle, leaving a sequence of marching camps which had fortified the places where they rested. The conquest was consolidated by the building of roads. The Pennines were bracketed by two great highways, the one in the west running from Chester to Carlisle while the one in the east had branches from Lincoln and York which united near Aldborough and

proceeded northwards to Scotch Corner. Between these major routeways were east–west link roads which traversed the hills and dales. Ilkley emerged as a route centre in the region, with roads radiating outwards to York, Aldborough, Bainbridge, Elslack and Manchester. Roman Ilkley or Olicana existed as a midway station between Manchester and York. Although Victorian development transformed the townlet, the lay-out of the Roman camp here is still preserved in the townscape and perpetuated in the playing-card-shaped block of land flanked by New Brook Sheet and containing the church.

The Roman fort of Virosidum stood on the drumlin overlooking Bainbridge

Towards the close of the second century a revolt by the northern tribes partly destroyed the Roman station at Ilkley. A large force of troops was despatched from Britain in AD 196 to bolster the bid for the imperial throne by Septimus Severus. Not only did this attempt fail but it also provided Scottish tribes, the Caledonii and Maeatae, with an irresistible opportunity to strike southwards, their offensive reaching as far as Ilkley and York. Between 200 and 210 the garrison at Ilkley was rebuilt by the battalion-sized cohort of the Lingones stationed there. There is an interesting possibility that these soldiers may have been able to converse with the local Brigantian tribesmen, for the Lingones were Celtic-speakers from the Champagne district of France.

More than thirty miles (48 km) of potentially hostile country separated Ilkley from the Roman fort at Bainbridge in Wensleydale, the road between the two outposts of the civilised world following the valley of the Ribble. The Bainbridge fort, known as Virosidum, stood upon the tip of a glacial hill or drumlin which overlooks the present village. The first fort here was built by the troops of Agricola a few decades after the invasion of Britain. The invasion of AD 196–7 or a previous revolt of northern tribesmen in AD 155 resulted in the earth and timber defences at Virosidum being rebuilt in stone. Sadly, although the outlines of the fortress can be traced in the turf, there is very little left to inspire visitors exploring the site of Virosidum except a fine view of the village below.

People living in the Dales did not become Romans when the forts were built at Ilkley, Bainbridge and Elslack, west of Ilkley, any more than they became Americans after the sinister spy-station was built at Menwith Hill, near Harrogate. Many will have remained close to their homesteads and will never have seen a Roman or the tribesmen from Belgium, Holland, Germany, France, Spain, Yugoslavia and Romania who formed the bulk of the legions. Most must have heard tales of the fabulous fortress and city at York (Eburacum), but the main effect upon their lives concerned the imposition of a reasonably reliable peace and the creation of a commercial market for whatever surpluses they may have been able to win from the land. The picture of Brigantia as a dark forest seething with rebel tribesmen is a false one. Most of the forest had gone and the majority of people were hill farmers – and would remain so for a very long time.

The final third of the Roman occupation saw a periodic breakdown in the security of the colony. Firstly, the naval commander Carausius and then his assassin, Allectus, made bids for the throne. Allectus withdrew troops from the north and fought an unsuccessful battle against Constantius in the south of England in 296. Again the northern tribes exploited the weakness in the empire and struck southwards. During troubled times such as these the more prosperous members of the Dales community saw their settled world disintegrating. Roman coins dating from AD 253–340 found in Victoria Cave and Dowkerbottom Cave reflect the insecurities of the times. Were they hidden here by folk of substance who were never able to reclaim their hoards or were they the plunder of raiders who likewise failed to return?

In 407 Constantius III withdrew the last of the legions from Britain, for Rome itself was under threat. For some time the stability of society was preserved and when it crumbled the Dales suffered far less than the lowlands, which had prospered under Roman rule and grown accustomed to the luxurious trappings of civilised life. In the Dales the Roman legacy was not a great one: a few crumbling forts and roads which probably existed as tracks before the conquest and would be so again when the tramp of the patrols was heard no more.

Attempts by Romanised aristocrats to preserve the unity of the British realm failed and the former colony gradually fragmented into autonomous provinces. To the south of our region a strong Celtic kingdom, known as Elmet, developed around Leeds and it is thought that a kingdom of Craven was formed in the Dales. Gradually, however, the political initiative passed from the British to the English or Anglo-Saxons. Though relatively few in numbers, these immigrants from the Low Countries and Denmark seem to have been better able to adapt to the hardships and turmoils of the times. They may have filtered into the Dales as soldiers or brigands, but will have come mainly as a trickle of humble farmers looking for footholds in the landscape of field and commons. In 617 the English-led army of King Edwin of Northumbria conquered the kingdom of Elmet and, although Celtic dialects would continue to be spoken in the Dales for many years to come, the region was now destined to become an English-speaking land.

New settlers speaking new languages were to follow. Viking raids became a serious threat to coastal communities at the end of the eighth century and in the one that followed raiding gave way to permanent settlement and conquest. In 866 Ivan the Boneless sailed a fleet up the Ouse to take the Northumbrian capital of York. While the Danes were consolidating their grip on the English lowlands, Norwegian Vikings, the Norse, had established an empire of bases and trading centres running from Orkney down the western seaboard of Scotland and around the Irish Sea. From Lancashire and Cumbria landless Norse settlers penetrated the Dales from the west while in 919 York was taken by the Norwegians. In the Dales Danish farmers who had followed the rivers into the region from their York or 'Jorvik' kingdom settled alongside Norse colonists who had moved in from the opposite direction.

Thus in the century before the Norman Conquest the Dales contained a strong element of native British people with a deep ancestry in the region, English-speaking Saxon families, Norse folk and Danes. The different Scandinavian elements would have been able to understand each other with difficulty and would have recognised little more than the odd word or phrase of the English dialect: the Celtic and Germanic speakers had very few words in common. And so in the Dales, whenever the speakers of Old English, Old Norse and Old Danish met, outside their farmsteads, on the tracks or at the market, they had to evolve a form of pidgin English which could serve as a lingua franca. This led to the simplification of Old English, with its complicated inflections and the inclusion of many Scandinavian words. In the Lake District to the north-west the Celtic language survived into the early Middle Ages but in the Dales it seems to have died before the Norman Conquest. And yet it still lives all around us, enduring in the names of natural features of the landscape. One can imagine the Germanic speakers asking the names of the hills and rivers that they saw during their explorations of the Dales, learning the names and then handing them down.

Examples of the Celtic names include the River Ure, meaning 'strong or holy river', the River Nidd, 'brilliant or shining river', and the River Wharfe, named after a Celtic goddess. Not all river-names remained Celtic; the Rivers Ribble and Swale have Old English names, the former translated as 'the tearing one' and the latter 'the rushing river'. As I pointed out at the start of this book, 'dale' is a Danish word, but sometimes the Danish and Celtic words were combined, as in Nidderdale, the dale of the Nidd. There was no rule governing which name should survive and which would be replaced. Peny-y-ghent is an obviously Celtic survival, but its lofty neighbour Ingleborough has an English name. It is 'Ingeld's fortress', a reference to the ancient hillfort, while Ingeld probably had an estate here, for Ingleton nearby is 'Ingeld's farm'. The 'Pen' in Pen-y-ghent is an element which occurs in so many Celtic place-names and means 'head', but the range of which this mountain is a part does not have a Celtic name. The word 'Pennines' was not used before the eighteenth century – it seems to have been invented by one William Bertram around the middle of that century.

Just as the Old Danish, Norse and English speakers once lived cheek by jowl, so today we find the names that they gave to places jumbled together in the countryside. Most of the books suggest that because a village has, say, an Old Norse name, then it was founded by Norsemen. This is nonsense; it might only have been renamed by them after decades or centuries of previous existence. Also, many village-names clearly show that no village

ABOVE
Yockenthwaite hamlet exemplifies the age-old settlement pattern of the Dales and its name combines both Danish and Celtic words; it is the meadow belonging to the Celt, Eogan

OPPOSITE
At shows and livestock markets in the Dales one can meet the descendants of farmers who settled here thousands of years ago

existed when the name was given, so that when it grew the village adopted the name of the place at which it appeared. Long Preston in Ribblesdale, for example, was the priest's farmstead that later grew into a long village, and Hellifield, a couple of miles away, was a field belonging to a Norse landowner called Helgi.

Place-names in forgotten languages are sprinkled generously across the map of the Dales and there is no English region with a richer or more varied endowment. Each of these names meant something at the time when it was given and usually they tell us something of the countryside of a thousand years ago. Streams here are known either as gills or becks, both these words having Norse origins. Occasionally the Anglo-Saxon word for stream, 'burn', will appear in a name, like Otterburn, and more rarely still, a Celtic stream word survives, as in Dacre in Nidderdale. Steep hillsides in the Dales are generally known as 'banks' but sometimes the Norse 'cliffe' is still used, or less commonly the Norse 'brekka' or the Danish 'brink'. Arncliffe, in Littondale, has a name meaning 'eagle slope', recalling distant times when eagles must have nested on the nearby scars. As in many other parts of England, village names often end in the Saxon 'ham', 'ton', 'ingham' and 'ington' endings, which just denote small settlements or farmsteads. Almost as common are the Norse 'by' and Danish 'thorpe' endings, which also refer to farmsteads and hamlets. Often too these endings are preceded by a personal name which may commemorate the Dark Age patriarch who established or held the settlement. Other place-names also include personal names, like Godwinscales in Nidderdale, which denotes Godwin's summer settlement. Summer settlements were frequently used as the herdsmen and shepherds left their winter homes to live among their cattle and sheep which grazed the summer pastures of the high fells and secluded valleys. 'Sett' is another name ending which denotes the sites of summer huts.

Most interesting of all are the names which describe how the countryside used to be and what it was used for. Yeadon in Nidderdale was once the valley where the yew trees grew, while Swinden in Ribblesdale was the valley of pigs – perhaps they were led out by the swineherd to forage beneath the oaks? Names change through time, so that what was in medieval times the 'Fouleshagh' or dirty (swampy?) copse evolved to become Foldshaw and might wrongly by linked to a sheep fold. Translations can also be a matter for debate, so that Arncliffe might not be the bank of the eagles but the bank which could be crossed by a horseman.

It might help interested visitors to understand the Dales if the old history books and some of the newer ones were burned. There is little reason if any to suppose that Briton, Saxon and Viking fought bloody battles in the Dales. Far better to imagine them evolving a dialect in which they could communicate, helping each other out at harvest and with the newcomers winning wives from among the indigenous communities. Within a short time the valleys were populated not by Celts or Saxons or Norsemen but by Dalesfolk. If the genocidal conflicts imagined by the old historians had really taken place, life in the defenceless hamlets and farmsteads which characterised the Dales since the dawn of farming simply could not have endured.

Villages are also the subjects of much myth-making. There were very few fully fledged villages in the Dales before the Middle Ages. This was – and to some extent still is – a countryside of solitary farmsteads and little cottage groupings. Parishes could be vast, often too large to make churchgoing a practical possibility for scores of households, so more important than the parishes were the smaller townships composed of groups of farms and hamlets. Were one to have asked a Dales farmer of the Dark Ages where he was from he would have replied with the name of his township.

Much is still to be learned about the homes of the Dalesfolk as they existed before the Norman Conquest. The best clues come from the excavation of a farmstead of about 870 at Ribblehead on the northern flank of Ingleborough. The farmstead and its outbuildings stood beside little paddocks on a limestone shelf now almost denuded of soil. The main building was elongated rather in the manner of a Viking longhouse, with low boulder and rubble walls and a tall gabled roof of thatch. Fragments of a variety of metals were found by the excavators, suggesting that metalworking here was more a cottage industry than a form of self-sufficiency. Even so, had the buildings been circular rather than rectangular and elongated the site would be indistinguishable from that of a Celtic settlement of 1000 years before. Through times of plenty and times of crises families moved on and settlers came to take their place. But, whatever the details in the story, the Dalesfolk trod in the footsteps of their forebears. They faced the same challenges and found the same answers. I know that when I was a boy there were men around my own village who stood infinitely closer to the folk who farmed at Ribblehead a thousand years ago than they would stand to the modern whizzkids of the enterprise culture.

CHAPTER 4

The Normans in the Dales

Within a day or two of the event Dalesfolk will have learned that the army of King Harold had defeated an invasion force led by the Viking Harold Hardrada and Tostig, the brother of their English King, at Stamford Bridge near York. Most will have been pleased by the outcome, for Earl Tostig was known as a harsh and murderous ruler during his overlordship of the north. They may also have learned that the royal army and the southern levies had marched to confront another invasion force led by William of Normandy. Just a few of them may have headed southwards to help the King, but it was October and there was work to be done before winter laid its grip on the land. Better to stay at home, if need be to face the seemingly greater threat of invasion by the Scots.

The news which filtered north from the battlefield at Hastings was less welcome though perhaps not regarded as disastrous. Harold was not a man of the north and who could be sure that William's rule could be extended beyond the Trent or Humber? If loyalty was owed to anyone it was to the homegrown lords, like Gospatric and Gamelbar, and the northern earls, Edwin and Morcar, who had led an army defeated at Fulford near York before the southern forces turned the tide of battle at Stamford Bridge. Two years after the Norman Conquest Edwin and Morcar turned against the new King and William's forces marched north to fortify York. Then a revolt flared in the north-east, where an army attempting to install a new Norman earl was annihilated, while in Yorkshire Edgar Atheling of the royal line of Wessex was proclaimed King in York. When a Danish army sailed up the Humber the Vikings were not attacked as invaders but welcomed as allies.

William acted swiftly, bribing the remaining Danes to leave and riding northwards at the head of his cavalry. He then enacted a systematic

The Norman keep tower at Richmond

campaign of genocide which left the villages in flames and the roads littered with the corpses of men, women and children. The terrible carnage was described by the chronicler, Orderic Vitalis, who wrote within living memory of the massacres:

> In his anger he commanded that all crops and herds, chattels and food of every kind should be brought together and burned to ashes with consuming fire, so that the whole region north of the Humber might be stripped of all means of sustenance. In consequence so serious a scarcity was felt in England, and so terrible a famine fell upon the humble and defenceless population that more than 100,000 Christian folk of both sexes, young and old alike, perished of hunger.

Another chronicler, Simeon of Durham, described how the land lay desolate for nine years and how the starving survivors were reduced to eating dogs and cats while packs of dogs and wolves tore at the corpses of those who died: 'For nobody survived to cover them with earth, all having perished by the sword and starvation, or left the land of their fathers because of hunger. . . . Between York and Durham no village was inhabited.' After the Norman forces had left the land smouldering and sodden with blood William's vassal, King Malcolm of Scotland, invaded to continue the slaughter and burning before returning to Scotland with the booty and hundreds of English slaves.

The Norman Harrying of the north of 1069–71 set the stage for the medieval developments in the Dales. Its effects must still be evident in the countryside for in many places the canvas of rural life was wiped bare. The land was parcelled out between William's leading supporters. Alan the Red of Brittany gained estates forfeited by the English Earl Edwin in 1069 and held a great tract of land around Richmond, Swaledale and Wensleydale. The King's half-brother, Robert, Count of Mortain, held 215 estates in Yorkshire, mainly to the east of Richmond. Roger de Poitou had extensive estates around Settle while Gilbert Tyson, the great standard-bearer, held lands between Skipton and Knaresborough.

In 1086 the King commanded that Domesday Book should be compiled. The picture which it gives of the Dales at this time is a skimpy and sorry one. Of the 639 estates in the North Riding of Yorkshire some 217 were still described as 'waste' and 150 were partially waste. We do not know exactly how the meaning of the word was interpreted at the time and it is hard to imagine that lands were still lying vacant and derelict almost two decades after the Harrying. Even so it is clear that the old English and Scandinavian class of landowners was eliminated and that the fabric of life in the countryside was torn and tattered. The Normans and their continental allies were now the leaders of society, men who could not speak the language of the region and cared little for the well-being of their bondsmen. Some of them held estates both in the Dales and in the more fertile plains of the Vale of York, and it has been suggested that families were herded out of the Dales to repopulate the devastated villages of the Vale.

Though crippled and helpless after the Harrying, Yorkshire still had to be fortified, for the region existed as a border-zone of the Norman realm which was exposed to Scottish and Viking invasion. In the Dales there are few traces of the small earthen motte and bailey castles built to pacify the local peasantry, for such peasants were already cowed or killed. But there was a need for strategic centres. Tough and loyal followers of the King were installed in holdings known as 'castellanies' which guarded the Pennine passes and the western approaches to the Vale of York. Land to the north of the Ribble was absorbed into Roger de Poitou's great Honour of Lancaster while to the east a large holding focused on Richmond was created, where a formidable Norman castle was begun as soon as the Harrying ended.

Alan the Red's Honour of Richmond was a vast empire of estates containing 440 manors, with 199 manors and 43 outlying properties in Yorkshire and the remainder disposed across the kingdom. The role of the castle, which stood on a bluff high above the Swale, was to control the routeways entering the Vale of York from Scotland. The castle, built by Alan and almost complete by the time of his death in 1089, followed an unusual design and consisted of a large triangular enclosure or Great Court. One side was defined by the steep face of the bluff and this was defended only by a stockade; the other two sides were guarded by massive curtain walls of stone. The eastern wall drew least advantage from the terrain and was studded with three square projecting wall towers, a remarkably advanced innovation in military engineering. The gateway to the castle was at the apex furthest from the river and was guarded by a two-storeyed gatehouse.

The domestic life of the castle was conducted in a building known later as Scolland's Hall, which still survives – the only other enduring example of an eleventh-century castle hall being at Chepstow. It is a two-storeyed building with the great hall, where all the public functions of the castle were conducted, occupying the upper floor and the space below used for cellarage.

A town developed below the great fortress and the street name 'French-gate' suggests that an alien population was attracted to the Norman focus. Bitter memories of Alan's rule may have been passed down through the generations, to surface in an old local rhyme which seems to mock the alien ways of the Breton lord and the entourage of carpet-baggers which he introduced. It is said he:

> Came out of Brittany
> With his wife Tiffany
> And his maid Manfras
> And his dog Hardigras.

For many years Richmond Castle was tough and remarkably advanced, yet not a great landmark. Exactly a century after work was begun it passed to Henry II, who was acting as guardian to the heiress (it remained with the Breton family until 1399), and work was begun on the great keep tower. This was built in an unusual position and incorporated in its footings the basement of the original gatehouse. The square tower has three floors and a battlement stage and it was a purely defensive addition to the defences, for the old Scolland's Hall continued to serve as the domestic, social and administrative focus. Visible for miles around, the keep tower still serves as a potent symbol of the Norman subjugation of the Dales.

Simultaneously Henry's engineers and bondsmen were engaged upon raising the keep at Bowes. This is another unusual castle. It was built to guard the old York-to-Carlisle routeway and was sited at the foot of the Stainmore Pass. As though to recall a previous era of conquest and pacification it actually stands within the defences of the Roman fort of Lavatrae. Bowes also lay in the domain of Alan the Red, who may have improved the old Roman defences, but Bowes is unusual in being a substantial stone keep which had little in the way of outer defences or ancillary buildings. Nor was it intended to provide much in the way of domestic comforts and diversions, being a military outpost which protected the Honour of Richmond against invasion by the Scots. It stood some 50 feet (15 m) tall and measured 82 feet (25 m) by 60 feet (18 m) in plan, a rugged, unadorned castle standing in countryside which is similarly uncompromising.

A Norman castle of quite a different nature can be explored in Wensleydale, at Middleham. Here was an estate which was part of the empire of Alan the Red. In 1086 Alan gave this and seven other manors to his brother, Ribald, who decided to fortify the site, and an earth-and-timber motte and bailey castle was erected some distance to the south-west of the present castle site. The remains survive as William's Hill and exemplify a type of castle much more numerous in most other parts of England than in the Dales. The fortunes of the dynasty rose and late in the twelfth century Robert Fitz-Ralph celebrated his status by commencing work on a new castle in stone, a castle which will have impressed its guests more than its enemies, for higher ground overlooks the chosen site.

The design favoured was that of the 'hall keep', of which Colchester and Castle Rising in Norfolk are the most celebrated examples. The advantage of this pattern is that it allows for more domestic space than do the more popular tall and narrow keep towers, like the one at Richmond. The adoption of a broad and squat design provided a floor space of around 9000 square feet (835 sq. m), about three times the amount available in the typical keep. The castle must have been surrounded by outer defences of some kind; a ditch survives but other outworks have been obliterated by the growth of the townlet of Middleham. Late in the thirteenth century a massive curtain wall was built around the keep. It is 4 feet 6 inches (1.3 m) thick, although only one substantial wall tower was provided. Like the keep itself it seems to have been created more to impress visitors than to intimidate attackers. During the fourteenth and fifteenth centuries a gatehouse was added to the north-east of the curtain and additional domestic buildings were added to the inner face of the wall. These provided private apartments for the ladies of the castle, offices and baking, milling and brewing facilities.

Middleham Castle has plenty to fascinate the visitor. However, because the curtain and the ancillary buildings attached to it encircle Robert Fitz-Ralph's castle so tightly it is not easy to form a clear impression of the appearance of the old hall keep. Perhaps as its makers intended, the castle was associated more closely with the great names than with the great battles of history. In 1270 it passed by marriage to another of the great northern dynasties, the Nevilles, and to Richard, Earl of Warwick, the Kingmaker. From Middleham Warwick plotted the downfall of Edward IV, who was imprisoned here. Later Richard, Duke of York, married Ann Neville, Warwick's daughter, and Middleham Castle was a part of her inheritance. It was from Middleham that Richard rode southwards in 1483 to become

Richard III, the last English and last Plantagenet King and, some believe, a much maligned monarch.

Middleham Castle

Other castles in the Dales did not undergo a transition from a construction in earth and timber to stone and were gradually overgrown and then forgotten. Some existed only briefly, like the earthwork castle at Hutton Conyers (apparently built to extort tribute from the townsfolk of Ripon), which was reduced by Henry II as he imposed order on an anarchic realm. At Skipton there is a massive stone castle which has engulfed and obliterated the traces of its Norman original. A little after 1086 the lands here were granted to Robert de Romille and a castle was built on a rock-girt site overlooking that on which the town would grow. This placing allowed it to command two ancient routeways and the Aire gap through the Pennines. During Norman times the palisaded mound and bailey may have been replaced by a castle of stone but the site was transformed at the start of the fourteenth century when towers and a curtain wall were built by Robert de Clifford, soon to be slain at Bannockburn. Further transformation took place in Tudor times when ranges of domestic buildings were built against the inner face of the curtain, while after the Civil War the Parliamentarians 'slighted' the castle, unroofing the buildings and greatly reducing the walls.

A royal castle sited on a high river bluff at Knaresborough guarded the mouth of Nidderdale and established the King's presence in an area prone both to insurrection and to Scottish invasion. As at Skipton the Norman traces are few and the first evidence of a castle dates from 1130, when £11 was spent on the 'King's works' here. The remains of the great medieval castle which developed are no longer impressive but derive from the building of a keep, curtain wall and wall towers in the middle years of the fourteenth century.

With the estates of the old English or Anglo-Danish lords fortified and the population reduced by the Harrying and famine, the Dalesfolk must have regarded the dawn of the Middle Ages with pessimism and trepidation. Their lords now had foreign names, foreign ways and spoke a foreign tongue. There was no longer a bond of loyalty or kinship between master and man and as the new castles rose so all hopes of change must have crumbled. Gradually the survivors rebuilt their lives, adjusted to the new forms of feudalism and tackled a new chapter in the story of the countryside.

CHAPTER 5

The Dales in the Middle Ages

At the start of the Middle Ages the Yorkshire Dales must have been more thinly peopled than it had been during the Roman or Iron Age periods. Domesday Book tells of a patchy countryside, here some peasants guiding the plough or guarding their stock and there estates lying derelict or still crippled from the Harrying. But in the Middle Ages, no less than before, land was the key to life, position and power. It could not be abandoned for too long. The Conquest had evicted the native aristocrats and replaced them with hard men who had clear ideas about the requirements of a feudal lord. Such a man needed working manors to create his wealth and provide his comforts, and he also needed tracts of hunting land where he and his guests could revel in the Norman passion for bloodsports.

Much of the poorer and some of the better land in the Dales was devoted to hunting, although the extents of the early hunting forests and chases is often unclear. Some of them may have been hunted in the Saxon era. There was a difference between the royal forests, which were controlled by the monarchs and where the severe and widely detested Forest Law was enforced, and the chases, where the greater nobles and churchmen had hunting rights. The Lords of Richmond had great chases in Arkengarthdale and the New Forest area of Swaledale.

Langstrothdale was the domain of the mighty Percy family, although in 1220 the ownership of the hunting rights was disputed by a Percy tenant, William de Arches, whose attempts to set himself up as the forester were scarcely judicious. In fact the story of the forests in the Dales is littered with litigation about matters large and small.

Knaresborough Castle was the administrative centre of a great royal forest. The oldest-surviving record of this forest dates from 1167, but the

49

forest will have been older than this. It covered most of lower Nidderdale and endured as an entity into the eighteenth century. The forests were not blanketed in woodland but contained fields, commons and populations of peasants – all subject to the oppressive game lords. Parts of the forests might be leased out to lay lords and no monarchs ever visited all the forests that they controlled. For example, no king is ever known to have hunted in the Forest of Bowland – though Henry VI was himself hunted there following the defeat of his Lancastrian army at Hexham in 1461. He may not have been too sorry to have been captured, for his main refuge was Bolton Hall, the home of Ralph de Pudsay, whose three marriages produced twenty-five children.

The forests and chases of the Dales must have curbed the growth of farming in the region and certainly imposed injustices upon the peasants, who could not drive the deer from their fields and were often burdened with obligations to serve the hunt. At the same time they also created employment and new settlements. In 1227, for example, it was claimed that the village of Bainbridge had earlier been founded to accommodate twelve foresters, each being awarded a house and a 9-acre (3.6-ha) plot of land. Each bailiff or warden had a large staff of foresters, regarders, agistors and woodwards who were variously responsible for supervising the adminis-tration of the forest, controlling poaching, grazing on pasture, acorns or beech mast, felling and the sale of holly branches as winter fodder. Bee-keepers pillaged the nests of wild bees for wax and honey and peat was

The village of Buckden was founded to house foresters employed by the Percy family in their chase of Langstrothdale

The ruins of Jervaulx Abbey

cut for fuel. The hunting industry was a big one. The Forest of Knaresborough was vast, about 20 miles (32 km) by 8 miles (13 km) with its own great courts and hierarchy of officials, while the relatively small manor and chase of Barden in Wharfedale covered 3252 acres (1316 ha) and that of Skipton some 15,360 acres (6216 ha).

In addition to the forests and chases there were the more compact deer parks, which were bounded by ditches and palings built in such a way that incoming deer were trapped until the day of the hunt, when they were released and pursued across the surrounding countryside. At the height of the popularity of the deer park in the thirteenth century there were sixty-seven examples in the North Riding. Being created mainly at a time when the recovery of peasant farming was gaining strength, the deer parks were widely disliked. One of the largest and most unpopular examples was Haverah Park near Knaresborough, which was created out of common land by William de Stuteville in 1173 and covered 2250 acres (910 ha). It was a favoured resort of several monarchs when in the north, including John, Edward I, Edward II and Edward III. Between their visits prosecutions against poachers were numerous, reflecting the continuing local resentment. Edward III established a renowned horse-breeding farm in the park, anticipating the trend to put the hunting reserves to more profitable uses. In Skipton Park, however, the Keeper of the Castle, Richard Oyset, was found to have gone too far. In 1307 the park contained seventy mares and only a dozen deer. The same inquisition found that timber had been felled and sold to iron forges and other customers.

The Dales had attractions to men more pious than the warlike huntsmen. Once the north had boasted a fine array of Benedictine houses but this early monastic tradition was rent apart by the Viking raids, and north of the Trent it perished. However, after the Norman conquest Reinfrid, one of William's knights, took monastic vows and succeeded in re-establishing monastic life at Jarrow, Monkwearmouth, Whitby and York. At first it appeared that the monastic revival would be accomplished by members of the venerable Benedictine order, or by the Cluniacs, reformed Benedictines who enjoyed royal favour. But in 1132 Rievaulx Abbey was established as a Cistercian house. The Cistercians reacted against the affluence and arrogance of the Cluniac monks much as the monks of Cluny had opposed the Benedictines. Expanding from the parent house at Citeaux in Burgundy, they had founded their first English house at Waverley in Surrey in 1128. The emphasis of their rule was on a life of austerity and toil rather than scholarship and ritual, so it is not surprising that members of the Order gravitated to the north.

The example of the Cistercians at Rievaulx probably encouraged Benedictine monks at the wealthy abbey of St Mary's in York who were offended by the slackness of discipline there. Led by Richard, the Prior, a group of thirteen monks appealed unsuccessfully to their Abbot. Then they invited Archbishop Thurstan to review their complaints, which led to a public fracas between the Archbishop and Abbot. Shielded by Thurstan, the dissidents stayed with him in his palace for three months. It was on what is now Boxing Day, the Feast of St Stephen, in 1133, when they walked with the Archbishop of Ripon along the River Skell that they saw, and were given, a piece of ground in which they could build their own monastery. At first they suffered extreme hardships but in 1135 they received money from Hugh, a dean of York, who joined the pioneers. An application to St Bernard, Abbot of Clairvaux, for enrolment in the Cistercian order was successful and their abbey of St Mary *ad fontes* grew to become the most renowned of all Cistercian foundations. Now it is known as Fountains Abbey, and its influence upon the Dales has been profound.

The Cistercians had great Yorkshire abbeys at Meaux, near Hull,

Kirkstall, near Leeds, Rievaulx and Byland, to the east of our region, and in the Dales at Jervaulx and Sawley. Other monasteries in the Dales were the Premonstratensian houses at Easby near Ripon and Coverham in Wensleydale, an Augustinian priory at Bolton in Wharfedale and a house of Benedictine nuns at Marrick, near Richmond.

Several of these foundations are associated with romantic legends, which one may or may not choose to believe. Jervaulx was established in 1156 and the old records tell that the first Abbot-to-be, John de Kinstan, and twelve monks were travelling out from Byland Abbey when they became lost in a dense wood. They were guided to safety by a vision of the Virgin and Child and were told, 'You are late of Byland but now of Yorevale.' Yorevale was Wensleydale and it was transcribed into the French of the time to become Jervaulx. A more reliable, if less romantic, version of the story sees Jervaulx being founded by monks from a daughter house of Rievaulx in Fossdale, the monks abandoning Foss because of the harshness of the climate and the ravages of wolf packs. Jervaulx grew to become a typically independent Cistercian Abbey and gained control of half of Wensleydale.

Bolton Priory boasts its own mythology. Legend tells that the boy Romilly, heir to the lordship of Skipton, had been hunting in the Barden area of Wharfedale and was returning with a forester when they attempted to cross a tumultuous little gorge on the Wharfe known as the Strid. As Romilly jumped the Strid, the greyhound which he was leading faltered and the boy was drowned in the charging waters. To commemorate the tragedy Alicia and William FitzDuncan, the grieving parents, donated the site of Bolton Abbey to the monks of Embsay. The monks knew the value of a good yarn which glamorised their history but a more sober version of the facts relates that Augustinian Canons came here around 1145 after attempts to found a daughter house of Huntindon Priory at Embsay had failed because of the poverty of the resources there. Bolton gained independence from Huntindon in 1194 and experienced a history of crises resulting from extravagance, debt, disease and Scottish raiding.

Despite these troubles the canons of Bolton were more popular among the Dalesfolk than the Cistercians. The order had been founded to introduce a firmer discipline among the canons, who became involved in the day-to-day life of the region and provided clergy for many of its churches. Another reforming order was that of the Premonstratensian canons, though its members became more introspective than the Augustinian canons. Though the site is picturesque and the ruins are quite impressive and lie very close to Richmond, the Premonstratensian Easby Abbey is less well known than Jervaulx or Bolton. It was founded by Roald, Constable of Richmond, in 1151 to accommodate thirteen canons and was enlarged in 1392. It suffered through its position close to routeways between England and Scotland and was not only pillaged by Scottish raiding parties

OVERLEAF LEFT
Bolton Priory

OVERLEAF RIGHT
ABOVE
The great cellarium at Fountains where the harvest of fleeces was stored

BELOW
The village of Kilnsey originated as a grange of Fountains Abbey

but also looted and damaged by English soldiers prior to the Battle of Neville's Cross in 1346. At the dissolution of the abbeys the canons of Easby, apart from the Abbot, did not receive pensions like many other monks and are said to have been hanged for resisting the suppression. The Premonstratensians also occupied an abbey in Coverdale at Coverham which was founded in the thirteenth century. It was severely damaged by the Scots in 1331, but recovered. The ruins, however, are small; they were pillaged long ago for stones to use in local houses and lie in private grounds.

The Cistercian abbey at Sawley was colonised from Newminster in Northumberland, itself a daughter house of Fountains which was established when Fountains was but seven years old. Sawley never became a major player in the great monastic land rush but despite its poverty it developed a fine reputation for scholarship and established a hospital for lepers at Tadcaster. It provides an example of how the Cistercian cause might have developed if wealth and power had not intervened. Marrick Priory, near Reeth, was founded for a community of Benedictine nuns in the twelfth century by Roger de Aske. At the dissolution a prioress and twelve nuns lived here. The ruins were robbed during the building of the church in the nineteenth century and later redeveloped as a youth centre attached to a farmstead.

As the English wool and then textile industries blossomed the lands in the north provided the source of vast fortunes to the monks. Some of the land granted to the abbeys was church land before the Conquest. Much more was given piecemeal by landowners hoping that salvation could be bought as the monks prayed for the souls of their benefactors. Gifts involved not only land but also the tithe incomes from parish churches which the landowners had controlled. Eventually about a quarter of the land in the Dales was linked to monastic houses, and Fountains had a million acres in the Craven region. Some abbeys outside the Dales also controlled important holdings, like Furness in Cumbria and Kirkstall. Fountains held estates beyond the Dales and disputed grazing rights in Borrowdale in the Lake District with Furness Abbey. Often the abbey estates had common boundaries, the lands of Fountains and Bolton meeting in the Malham area and those of Fountains and Byland joining in upper Nidderdale. The names of the monastic owners may still survive in the countryside, as with Fountains Fell, Prior Rakes, near Malham, and Fountains Earth in Nidderdale. Eventually some ten abbeys controlled land in the Dales, only two of them lying within the modern National Park boundary. Distant Bridlington Priory held much of Swaledale, just as Jervaulx controlled much of upper Wensleydale and upper Ribblesdale. Squabbles between the different monastic houses and between them and laymen were quite common. The monks of Fountains and Sawley squabbled violently over rights to a watermill in Littondale, while complaints that the monastic flocks encroached upon common grazings were frequent. Laymen holding land in the Dales were often of a tough and lawless breed and it was not unknown for monks to be ambushed and attacked. The monks, in turn, were quite capable of violence and found that what had begun as a quest for solitude and devotion had become very big business indeed. Wool was not the only commodity produced by the monks. Fountains and Byland exploited lead-mining and smelting in Nidderdale and the Roman lead-mines on Greenhow Hill were redeveloped, while Fountains also bred cattle at Bouthwaite, a few miles away. Bridlington developed iron-working in Swaledale and Jervaulx had small-scale iron and lead enterprises in Wensleydale. The Premonstratensians and Augustinians were enthusiastic livestock farmers, but the Cistercians were the leaders of the economic league. As the years passed, it would have become harder and harder to remember that their communities were founded to be self-sufficient, producing enough only to feed themselves and to support charity. The quest for wool-based wealth probably originated in ambitious monastic building projects, with flocks being expanded to meet the costs of the works. Most of the physical labour on the Cistercian estates was done not by the monks but by the semi-educated lay brothers who outnumbered them. In the middle of the twelfth century Rievaulx supported about 140 monks and well over 500 lay brothers, and the usual complement at Fountains was 30 to 40 monks and 200 lay brothers.

Each estate was divided into monastic farms or 'granges' and each grange was worked by a small team of lay brothers under the charge of a priest–monk. It usually had its own chapel and refectory as well as farm buildings. Some granges controlled outlying farms or lodges – the grange of Fountains at Kilnsey in Wharfedale oversaw some seven lodges in Langstrothdale. Close to the spectacular overhanging cliff at Kilnsey the hall of the old grange survives. The grange was founded after 1150 to manage extensive estates which the abbey had acquired in Craven and the track from Kilnsey to Fountains Fell endures as Mastiles Lane. Kilnsey was associated with the wool industry and with cutting thatching reeds from the former lake nearby, but abbeys had granges with other specialisations – horse-rearing at Horton in Ribblesdale and lead-smelting and iron-making at Brimham in Nidderdale. The Nidderdale hamlet of Smelthouses stands by the site of Brimham's old lead-smelter.

Much of the woolcrop was bought by Florentine and Venetian merchants who toured the monasteries and paid hard cash for the forthcoming wool-shearing. Soon the lay brethren became speculators, buying in wool from farmers and selling it along with the monastic quota. At the turn of the thirteenth century Fountains alone was producing up to 30,000 pounds (13,600 kg) of wool per year and one can gain an impression of the vast bulk of this production by exploring the gigantic cellarium which survives

at the abbey and which was built late in the twelfth century to store the fleeces. It is more than 300 feet (90 m) long. Despite the purity of their initial convictions and the steadfast manner in which they faced the hardship of founding their houses, the monks were soon behaving more as stockbrokers than as saints. Harmless peasant communities were evicted to make way for the granges of the expanding empires and, when Scottish raids threatened and frightened laymen took their valuables for 'safe keeping' to an abbey, they sometimes found that they were never returned. Even so, the monastic movement became enmeshed with life in the Dales. The monasteries provided clergy for many local churches and far-sighted folk feared that without the monks the way would be open for an influx of southern speculators. Thus in 1536 many Dalesfolk rebelled against the dissolution of the abbeys and joined the ill-fated Pilgrimage of Grace.

While the monks were organising and expanding their empires the peasants were also engaged in work which slowly changed the countryside. Abandoned farmland was reclaimed and as the farmsteads multiplied and the villages and hamlets swelled so new inroads were made into the forest. Land was needed for plough and pasture and timber was needed for building and as charcoal for the smelters. Sometimes the hunting interests attempted to check the encroachments but during the thirteenth century the ring of

Markenfield Hall near Ripon with its moat and gatehouse was built in the years after 1310; in 1318 the Scots burned nearby Knaresborough

The ridge-and-furrow patterns of medieval farming revealed during a snowmelt on slopes near Bolton Priory

the axe must have been more commonly heard than the shrill of the curlew. The woodland clearance or 'assarting' is commemorated in scores of place-names, like Riddings Hill between Bolton and Burnsall in Wharfedale or Rawridding in Dentdale, names which denote land rid of trees.

Places that had been desolate became overcrowded, but then the troubles returned. Today there is no antipathy between Dalesfolk and Scots. They have much in common and locate the source of their problems further south. In the Middle Ages, however, the Scots must have been despised. Scottish raiding had always been a threat but after the Scottish victory at Bannockburn in 1314 the raiders poured southwards. The town of Knaresborough was burned in 1318, despite the royal castle which overlooked it. Only 20 houses survived the flames and 140 were burned down. These threats coincided with the worsening of the climate and an eruption of blights. At Bolton Priory the waterlogging of the ground and the lack of hay caused the sheep flock to be reduced from over 3000 to under 1000. Then a Scottish army appeared in the locality and the Prior fled across the fells towards Blackburn. In the following year Archbishop Melton hastily assembled an army to resist a fresh Scottish invasion, but was vanquished at Myton on Swale near Ripon and the Dales lay exposed to further devastation. Yet another challenge loomed, for in 1319 a great cattle plague entered the Dales from the south. In 1320 this combination of adversities proved too much for the canons and Bolton Priory was abandoned. The monks found refuge in monasteries in the Midlands, though they returned five years later, invigorated, and undertook a great rebuilding of their church.

Worse was to follow. The Black Death arrived in southern England in 1348 and spread rapidly northwards. One might presume that, since the disease was spread by rats, the remote farmsteads and hamlets producing livestock rather than corn would have escaped. This may or may not have been so, but wherever the evidence exists it reveals a fearful death toll. Eight churchyards in the North Riding of Yorkshire were specially dedicated for plague victims and in the Forest of Knaresborough eight or nine people out of every twenty perished. The plague lingered for centuries to come, with terrible outbreaks in 1361–2 and 1374. In the eruption of the 1360s a third of the clergy in the deanery of Richmond and Catterick died and lesser folk will have fared no better. The plague still affected Shakespeare's England and the parish records of Horton-in-Ribblesdale show that in 1597 some seventy-four parishioners died (equal to one-eighth of the population), the average mortality in a normal year being fifteen.

In the latter part of the Middle Ages the Wars of the Roses gave rise to a new and more divisive form of conflict. Outsiders tend to imagine that this was a war between Yorkist Yorkshire and Lancastrian Lancashire, but this was far from being the case. The East and West Ridings were strongly Lancastrian and the North Riding, containing most of the Dales area, was divided. The Nevilles at Middleham and the Scropes at Castle Bolton were Yorkist, while the Cliffords of Skipton were Lancastrians. The division was the same among the lesser nobles, the Talbots being Yorkist and the Tempests, Singletons and Pudsays, all neighbours in the Forest of Bowland, being Lancastrians.

In 1513, however, the Dales families were able to unite against a common foe. In this year a sizeable force of tenants followed Henry, Lord Clifford, to Northumberland and the Scots were so soundly defeated at Flodden that raiding ceased to be a threat. In Arncliffe church the names of local people who fought at Flodden are preserved on the wall – an earlier list displayed there itemised their arms and mounts.

The early centuries of the Middle Ages witnessed the creation of forests, chases and parks and the establishment of monastic houses. In the end, however, it was the humble peasant, so often the victim of the great nobles and haughty churchmen, who left the firmer mark on the countryside. Under the pressures of a land-hungry population most of the hunting reserves withered away. The monasteries, meanwhile, never really recovered from the onslaught of the pestilence and in their quest for riches and power they had lost the goodwill of potential benefactors. In November

1539 the dissolution reached Fountains. The Abbot and thirty-one monks departed and Sir Richard Gresham bought their livestock: 1976 cattle, 1146 sheep, 86 horses and 79 swine. Sir Richard was the sort of man that northerners traditionally dislike – a London merchant and speculator – and he soon resold at a profit.

Henry VIII pioneered the trick of privatising other people's possessions for profit. The monastic estates tended to be bought by rich speculators, but in time the processes of reselling and selling again created a countryside of private estates, smaller freeholdings and agricultural tenancies, a pattern of life which evolves but persists. The widespread fears which had fuelled the Pilgrimage of Grace were well founded, for without the monasteries the churches of the Dales were stripped of clergy – in the West Riding there were nearly 900 clergymen on the eve of the dissolution but only 250 remained at the start of the reign of Queen Mary. Yet the monastic woollen industry had left its mark by stimulating a textile industry in the Dales. As early as 1379 the villages in Wharfedale upstream of Bolton Priory already supported thirteen tailors and eleven weavers, while a fulling mill had been established at Hebden Bridge.

CHAPTER 6

Village and Hamlet, Cross and Church

The region of the Yorkshire Dales contains many lovely villages, some too well known for their own good and tranquillity, and others lovely but less well known. In places like Gayle, Thwaite or Arncliffe it is hard to remember that the scene was not contrived as a film set for some movie remake of *Wuthering Heights* but is the product of humble toil and home-making. It is also ironic that while the area has a more than generous share of England's prettiest villages, the Dales was never real village country; the leading roles in the pattern of settlement were always played by the farmstead and hamlet.

Before we explore the story of the village it is worthwhile to look at the character of the Dales village landscape. Uninformed enjoyment of its prettiness can take one only so far; to derive more pleasure one must understand. What then are the features of the village scene which give it its essential personality? First, and most obviously, the dwellings and barns are built of the local sandstone, grit or limestone. Stone-laden carts could not travel too far along the steep and rutted hill tracks and stone for local building seldom moved more than two or three miles from the little village quarries. Consequently the buildings echo the hues and rough texture of the walls and bridges, which in turn echo the rocks exposed in the streambeds and scars. Secondly, there is the factor of age. The buildings in the unspoiled Dales villages tend to date from the late seventeenth to early nineteenth centuries. The movement for producing sturdy and durable homes which is known as the Great Rebuilding began in southern England in Tudor times but did not reach the Dales until much later. In the latter part of the nineteenth century several of the established industries of the Dales – like lead-mining and textiles – were in decline, so villages were

contracting rather than expanding. The surviving architecture of the Dales villages was largely built between these time brackets. Thirdly, unlike the situation in the flat Vale to the east, relatively few Dales villages seem to show the signs of medieval planning. As a result they have developed along winding tracks, through roads and back lanes so that undisciplined lay-outs of curving lines are common.

Most of the villages in the Dales have names which meant something in the Saxon or Viking languages, but this tells us little or nothing about the age of particular villages. If any of the villages have pedigrees which extend back before the Norman Conquest it is virtually impossible to prove the fact without large-scale archaeological excavations. Even after the Conquest the circumstances – with the spread of hunting reserves and the expansion of the monastic sheep runs – worked against village growth. Moreover, the countryside of steep slopes and bleak plateaux discriminated against the birth of villages. Lowland England had expanses of arable land to nourish open-field farming and the large villages of feudal peasants associated with it. But in the Dales ploughland was found in patches and pockets in the valleys and the age-old emphasis on livestock rearing favoured a thinner and more fragmented pattern of farming.

Villages, mainly small ones, did develop, but to develop they needed a special reason. They might be route and market centres, places which provided services to a nearby castle, foci for the administration of hunting forests or the bases for a local industry. I have mentioned that in 1227 Ranulph, son of Robert, claimed that his ancestors had founded Bainbridge to accommodate twelve foresters. The legend may be true since it is unlikely that a settlement had endured here since the times of the Roman fort. Other forest villages may have had similar origins, for each forest required a large staff of officials and servants.

Agricultural resources are spread thinly and to grow by developing as a trading centre a place needed certain advantages. Many villages in the Dales contain a crossroads and a bridge, assets which ensured more traffic than less favoured spots could exploit. For a legal market to be held a special charter was needed. The dates of most market charters in the Dales are known, but various villages could have been the venues for ancient customary markets before the legal stamp of approval was issued. Often the winning of a market charter would be followed by the creation of a new village lay-out; the triangular village green at the royal forest village of Hampsthwaite in Nidderdale almost certainly dates from the granting of a market and fair charter in 1304.

Market trading was a precarious business and the advantage of a head start did not guarantee success, as the example of Wensleydale, uncommonly well endowed with medieval markets, shows. The village of Wensley gained its charter in 1202 and Masham market was legalised in 1250. In

1305 Carperby gained a charter and East Witton was similarly endowed in 1307, while the village which had grown at the gates of Middleham Castle was chartered in 1387. In 1563 Wensley was afflicted by the Black Death and the oldest of the Dale's market centres never recovered its trade; it was lost to a new market established at Askrigg. Then Leyburn gained a market in 1684 and Hawes one in 1700, scooping much of the trade from the older trading centres, several of which had feudal origins and could not cope with change. Early market charters provided the foundations for the success of places like Settle, Sedbergh and Skipton, but could not underwrite the future of trading drop-outs like Grinton or Kettlewell. Pateley Bridge gained a market in 1324 but the improvement of road links to Ripon in the eighteenth century robbed the place of much of its trade. Then, as the demand for food in the fast-expanding industrial towns grew, dealers in farm produce began to tour the farms and the produce never came to market. In 1839 the market was said to be 'nearly at an end' but the lead and quarrying industries kept the townlet alive.

Some villages owed their status to medieval markets but there were others which derived from monastic granges. At first the monastic land rush had tolled the death knell for small village communities – like the long-lost village of Herleshow, snuffed out by the monks because it lay too near to the site of Fountains Abbey. Later in the Middle Ages there was a tendency for the monastic granges to be let out to lay tenants, and hamlets or farmsteads established around the old grange could grow to become villages. Examples include Kilnsey and most of the villages in upper Nidderdale, like Ramsgill, Lofthouse and Middlesmoor.

If agriculture could seldom sustain settlements larger than hamlets, industry sometimes could. At Alston, to the north of our region, a church and market were created in the middle of the twelfth century for a community of the King's miners. In other areas medieval industry did not tend to create compact and coherent villages. Later, however, such places did begin to gell under the stimulus of industry. The straggling settlement of Greenhow Hill, close to the ancient lead mines above Pateley Bridge, was formed in the seventeenth century so that miners were spared the arduous walk up to the workings; they were awarded cottages and smallholdings, could raise cattle and pigs and pasture their sheep on the moor.

Although most of the villages in the Dales did not originate as specialist industrial villages there are scores of villages which owed their expansion or survival to local industries – for example quarrying at Middlesmoor in Nidderdale and Skyrethorns in Wharfedale, spinning at Linton, knitting at Gayle. Flax and textile mills boosted the population of so many of the settlements as the water-powered phase of the Industrial Revolution gained momentum. Later industry gravitated to the coalfields and although this caused a sharp decline in the size and prosperity of many settlements in the

The large green at East Witton, provided to house a market granted in 1307

Dales it would also add new members to the village flock. Wharfedale and Nidderdale were relatively accessible to the growing industrial conurbations and textile magnates sought verdant footholds where they could enact the role of the rural squire. Birstwith in Nidderdale was created by the Greenwood dynasty of mill owners. In lower Wharfedale the development of the house and park at Harewood was accompanied by the destruction of old villages, the diversion of the Skipton-to-Knaresborough road and the building of a new showpiece village beside the new road. The Lascelles family at Harewood house had a background as ribbon merchants. Other settlements which were not created as estate villages were titivated according to the whims of their haughty masters. At Ripley in Nidderdale the titivation amounted to a complete rebuilding.

In only a few cases are the details of a long village history plainly deduced but some fascinating stories have emerged. East Witton in Wensleydale is one of the most picturesque of villages and it seems that the original village was some distance away. The site of the present village was developed in the years around 1307, when the monks of nearby Jervaulx Abbey gained the right to hold a Monday market and a cattle fair at Martinmas. To the south-east of this village are the churchyard and relics of the old church of St Martin, which was linked to the original village. The lay-out of the new village was apparently planned by the monks with dwellings set beside the long market green, which was orientated on the abbey and along an old Wensleydale routeway. Much later, when the village gained its imposing church, the building was set a little remote and to the Jervaulx side of the village on land taken from the old open ploughlands. The church was provided by the Earl of Aylesbury in 1809 to commemorate the jubilee of King George III. It was about this time that the whole village was rebuilt, and although the number of dwellings remained about the same as that recorded two centuries earlier, the new houses were of stone and were well built, and survive to be admired today.

Further up the dale is Castle Bolton, where the houses line an elongated rectangular green, one end of which is dominated by the castle. Early in the fourteenth century members of the powerful Scrope family obtained the right to build a fortified home here. The result was a splendid 'quadrangular palace castle' which still impresses visitors. It seems very likely that at the time when the castle was being built Sir Richard Scrope also provided the adjacent church and completely reorganised an existing hamlet on the site to produce the disciplined village of Castle Bolton with its green orientated along an old trackway. Greens are often regarded as the most archaic features of the village landscape, but wherever the evidence has survived they emerge as additions to the scene and frequently they were provided to accommodate a market. The old notion of the green as a safe haven for cattle does not seem to have much value in the Dales – though it just might apply to Arncliffe, where the lanes and tracks kink into the green in a way which suggests that efforts might once have been made to defend the approaches to it.

Villages in the Dales were not sited according to defensive considerations, despite the medieval threat of Scottish raiding and the lawlessness of many locals. These locals were not disgruntled feudal peasants but freemen belonging to the middle layers of society. They feuded with each other, waylaid travellers and attacked the abbey servants. Then, when the authorities attempted to restore the rule of law, they would, according to the Abbot of Fountains, 'go into dales and fells so that there may be no common law executed against them'.

The origins of many villages in the dales are vague and debatable. However, if we count those which are known to have resulted or grown from hamlets as a consequence of a medieval market charter, to have evolved from monastic granges or to have flourished in association with a particular old industry then a substantial proportion of questions are answered. In the flat vale and eastern upland of Yorkshire lost village sites abound. Most commonly these places perished in Tudor times, when the houses were torn down to create vast sheep-ranching areas. In the Dales lost villages are far scarcer although there are a few unusual cases like West End in the Washburn valley, drowned to create a reservoir in the 1960s. The region escaped the Tudor onslaught because villages and people were much thinner on the ground and the sheep were here already.

In the south and midlands of England the villages tend to be older, and so too do the churches. Even so the story of Christianity in the Dales is a long one – even if the degree of devotion was often less than it might have been. Christianity in England gained a foothold during the Roman occupation and the nature of its survival in the troubled centuries which followed is hotly debated. It is clear that a Celtic Christian kingdom of Elmet endured throughout most of the pagan centuries in the lands around Leeds and it is quite possible that a similar one existed in the Craven region of the Dales. The physical evidence of Dark Age Christianity in the Dales comes not from churches but from crosses.

As the forces of Christianity reclaimed the land the Dales lay in the marchlands between two churches. Paulinus, a disciple of the missionary Augustine, became the Bishop of York in the kingdom of Northumbria, which adopted Christianity in 627. While Northumbria had accepted the Roman Church, apostles of Celtic Christianity who had a base on Lindisfarne began missionary work on the mainland of northern England. In 663 a synod was convened at Whitby to judge the claims of the competing churches – and the destiny of the Church was settled in favour of the Roman cause.

The early work of conversion and worship was accomplished by missionary monks operating from monastic churches or minsters, not all of which can now be identified. Preaching crosses of carved stone were erected at sites designated for worship. Some may have been associated with Christian burial grounds or early timber churches and some may have been placed on the sacred sites of pagan worship, claiming them for the new religion. Most of these crosses are lost; some were incorporated in the walls or foundations of later churches and some survive *in situ* or in other places. The best-known crosses in our region are the three at Ilkley. The tallest of the trio is 8 feet (2.4 m) tall and each one is decorated with scroll work and with figures. Their history is mysterious; the two shorter crosses are believed to have been moved from their original settings to follow ignominious careers as gate-posts. Then for many years they stood in the churchyard of All Saints before being moved to more protected positions in the interior of the church. They date from the years AD 800–50.

Very little church architecture of the Saxon period is found in the Dales, a notable exception being the church of St Mary at Masham. The walls of the nave might be as early as the seventh or eighth century, while just outside there is the shaft of an elaborately carved cross of the ninth century, with figures in arcades, animals and the cast of an unidentified legend. No less interesting though rather more puzzling is the case of the church at

Middlesmoor in upper Nidderdale. Inside the church is the ancient St Chad Cross and the lofty site of the church and its curving churchyard walls may hint at a pagan sacred site commandeered for Christian worship. In legend the church is associated with St Chad, the seventh-century missionary and Bishop of York, and if the legends are true this must have been one of the earliest Christian foundations in the north.

Another legend holds that James the Deacon, who kept the flame of Roman Christianity still flickering after Paulinus was forced to flee from York in 633, established a community of worshippers at Finghall near Catterick. Apparently he taught them to sing in the manner of the Church in Rome. This was the site of a verifiable synod in 789 and the roots of Christianity could go deeper. At Hauxwell, nearby, there is a Saxon cross known as St James's Cross, while Finghall Church has a Saxon cross head.

Ripon, on the eastern margins of the Dales, was an inspiring religious focus. St Wilfrid abandoned the Celtic Church for the Benedictine code and became Abbot of a monastry here in 661. A fine tradition of scholarship developed but the monastery fell prey to Viking attacks and perished in 950. The library and paintings were lost. Swiftly, however, the Danes converted to Christianity. Evidence of this survives at Burnsall in Wharfedale in the form of a distinctive 'hog-back' grave cover, a block of stone serving as a house of the dead with a gabled roof carved to represent shingles which is clasped by animals at either end. Such hog-backs are associated with Scandinavian Christian burials, and a superb trio of examples can be seen at Brompton-in-Allertonshire Church near North-allerton.

As we shall see, a large portion of the churches of the Dales were built or rebuilt in a very distinctive style of the later Middle Ages. Older churches are not as numerous as in lowland England and many families lived so remote from churches that conventional Sunday worship was seldom possible. On some manors the Norman lords continued the older practice of creating an estate church, so that the manor became the parish. Parishes in the Dales could be vast and embrace a great cluster of the older townships. The church at Aysgarth served the whole of upper Wensleydale, and Grinton Church, staffed by priests from far-off Bridlington Priory, served all of upper Swaledale. As the monastic movement once more recovered, this time after the devastation wrought by the Harrying, many lands passed into monastic control but the relations between church and congregation varied greatly according to the monastic order concerned.

The Cistercians tended to remain aloof but the ordained priests who composed the Augustinian community at Bolton served several far-flung churches. Meanwhile distant Dereham Abbey in Norfolk provided the canons who served as priests at Kirkby Malham. This was because one Adam of Giggleswick had granted it to the abbey in 1199 – but the church at Giggleswick itself was controlled by the Benedictine monks of Finchale Priory near Durham. (Different Adams of Giggleswick donated the annual payment of 4od (17p) from land rented to Fountains to provide 'coverings for the heads of those infested with worms to be cured at the gate' of the abbey, where unfortunates queued for charity.)

The abbeys staffed the churches of the Dales and in a few cases they provided chapels for their tenants. The Augustinian monastic churches tended to survive the dissolution because, as at Bolton, their naves were shared with lay worshippers. In Nidderdale churches at Bewerley and Ramsgill were provided by the abbeys of Fountains and Byland respectively.

One of the older churches in the Dales is at Linton in Wharfedale. It was the church of the manor of Linton and this link was underlined in the fourteenth century when the lord, Sir John le Gras, appointed three of his relatives in succession as parson! The situation here was unusual, for not only did the church serve three villages apart from Linton – Grassington, Hebden and Threshfield – but also the right to appoint the rector became divided, and the church was served by two rectors until 1866. One pier, several capitals and part of the chancel arch show that the building has Norman origins, although it has been argued that the detached riverside situation indicates a much earlier church established on a pagan sacred site. Work of the thirteenth and fourteenth centuries predominates; there is no tower and the humble bell turret is thought to have been built in the thirteenth century and repositioned in the fourteenth century.

The church of St Oswald at Horton-in-Ribblesdale has a beautiful setting, with Pen-y-ghent forming the distant backdrop. Rather more of the Norman legacy remains, including the nave arcades, the south door, with its 'dog-tooth' decoration, and a fine font embellished with chevron carving. At first the church was controlled and served by the monks of Jervaulx but following some ecclesiastical wrangles the right to appoint a priest was assigned to the nuns of Clemmenthorpe, near York. Medieval coloured glass rarely survives in the Dales but it can be seen in the west window where the Virgin Mary, Thomas à Becket and the arms of Jervaulx Abbey are depicted. The masonry beside the south door is grooved, probably as a result of arrow-sharpening work by medieval archers.

Churches so often embody the history of their parish and Saxon cross fragments, Danish tombs and Norman fonts whisper messages about the roots of Christianity. Similarly the imposing thirteenth-century church of the Holy Trinity at Wensley, with fine Flemish brass of the fourteenth century, seems rather grand for the present village and recalls times when the medieval market flourished here. Wensley is now dwarfed by nearby Leyburn, which grew much later and did not gain its church until 1868 nor its independence of Wensley until 1956. The church at Kirklinton, near Ripon, testifies to more dramatic events and is the result of a fourteenth-

century reconstruction following the destruction of an earlier church by Scots surging southwards after their victory at Bannockburn in 1314.

The medieval churches of the Dales tended to be small and thinly spread. A distinctive regional style of architecture did not emerge until the period had almost ended. The style which then arose seems perfectly tailored to the rugged landscapes and is now known as 'Pennine Perpendicular'. The 'Pennine' part obviously refers to the northern uplands, while the 'Perpendicular' was the national style which was adopted around the time of the Black Death. As epitomised in the great wool churches built in the south and midlands, often from the fortunes of the textile industry, the style embodied soaring vertical lines and vast window openings. In the northern Dales it was modified to account for the smallness of congregations, the paucity of rich patrons and the absence of high-grade freestone for building. Churches built in this manner often reveal a modest burst of wool-based prosperity but have long, low naves without chancel arches, battlemented towers which are far less ostentatious than in the south and shallowly angled roofs, often pitched low to reduce the heavy burden of roofing flags. Many of these churches post-date the Middle Ages and have flat-headed windows rather than the four-centred arches of the original Perpendicular windows. No other regional style of church building sits more comfortably into its surroundings.

One of the most rustic expressions of the Pennine Perpendicular can be seen at Hubberholme in Langstrothdale. The building dates from the fifteenth and sixteenth centuries though its roots go deeper, to a forest chapel which the Earl of Northumberland, William de Percy, gave to the monks of Coverham in 1241. A special treasure is a rare and ornate rood loft which is thought to have been pillaged from Coverham Abbey at the dissolution in 1548 (the church at Aysgarth contains a painted chancel screen taken from Jervaulx Abbey at the same time). Hubberholme epitomises the rugged nature of religious life in the Dales. During most of the medieval period it existed as a chapel of ease for Arncliffe in the next dale and had no rights of burial. This situation persisted until the late fifteenth century and the records tell of how eight bearers bound for Arncliffe almost perished in snowdrifts, while on another occasion the surging waters of the Wharfe swept a body from the grip of the mourners. To appreciate the fellowship binding the far-flung communities of the Dales we might ask ourselves whether we would be prepared to carry the body of a friend or relative placed in a flimsy wicker coffin for hours or for days across rough ground and uncontrolled rivers – and do this in the knowledge that there were no doctors, antibiotics or insurance schemes to help us should things go wrong. There is now a spirit abroad which insists there are no such things as society or community, but the old Dalesfolk had every reason to be glad that there were.

Corpse ways were used to carry bodies from remote corners of the parish to the church. We have seen that Linton Church served several villages and the tiny bridge nearby, known as Li'l Emily's Bridge, provided a link with Grassington and Threshfield. There is a fine church in the Pennine Perpendicular style at Grinton in Swaledale and it is linked to Keld by a corpse way which crosses the Ivelet Bridge. These half-forgotten tracks remind us of the realities of life in a thinly churched region. Today a traveller can breakfast at London King's Cross, comfortably take a high-speed train, a shuttle train and a number 24 bus and have lunch in Pateley Bridge. But around 1350 any worshipper from Bewerley near Pateley Bridge who wanted to visit his or her parish church rather than the local chapel of ease risked life and limb on the 8-mile (13-km) journey to Kirkby Malzeard. The Archbishop of York described people hereabouts as dwelling 'farre distant from anie parish church, to which for the swellings of waters and other tempest greatlie in winter season some men cannot passe without greate difficulties and corporall danger . . .'.

Kirkby Malham has a larger church in the local style but with echoes of the more grandiose Perpendicular manner of Norfolk. The Abbot of West Dereham in that county provided the vicars for Kirkby Malham and the building is largely the product of a rebuilding in the fifteenth century. Once more the parish served was vast and as at Hubberholme the entrance is slotted for an 'invasion beam' which could bar the door against Scottish invaders (the best English example of a fortified church tower is at Bedale on the eastern margins of the Dales). One more good example of the Pennine Perpendicular can be seen at Arncliffe, where there is yet another church dedicated to St Oswald, who invited the Celtic monks of Iona to send missionaries to the north of England. The Norman church was rebuilt and the tower at Arncliffe is of the fifteenth century. There was a restoration in the stark 'churchwarden Gothic' style at the end of the eighteenth century and a more sympathetic one in 1841. We have seen how Arncliffe buried the dead of Hubberholme and beyond, and another aspect of the remoteness of Christian life in the Dales is contained in the story of how, in about 1835, a certain William Boyd approached the Archbishop of York and asked to be installed as vicar at Arncliffe. It was only when the records of the diocese were dug out and perused that the Archbishop could be convinced that such a parish existed. Meanwhile the vicarage had been divided between a poor house and a wool store used by the local farmers. And yet isolation could have its advantages, for the diocesan edict of 1571 which demanded the destruction of 'popish' rood screens can never have reached forgotten Hubberholme.

After the Middle Ages the building of churches slowed down but did not stop. After the Reformation the choice of the 'wrong' form of worship could place Dalesfolk in danger, though often they followed the lead set by their

OPPOSITE ABOVE
*The lovely old church
at Horton-in-
Ribblesdale*

OPPOSITE BELOW
*The Pennine
Perpendicular style
displayed in the
remote church at
Hubberholme*

The church at Kirkby
Malham

masters. Thus the Catholic religion remained strong in the area dominated by the Ingilby family at Ripley Castle and the Scrope family at Bolton in Wensleydale. As the years passed various dissenting religions found support and in the mid-seventeenth century George Fox won many adherents to Quakerism. The monuments to this pure and simple faith are not obvious, but include a few meeting houses as at Skipton and a little Quaker graveyard at Hardcastle Garth near Darley in Nidderdale.

John Wesley preached in the Dales on numerous occasions between the 1740s and the 1780s and villagers and farmers will still point out the places where Dalesfolk flocked in their hundreds to hear the evangelist of Methodism. He was a great influence in Wensleydale and Swaledale and also visited the southern Dales, preaching in Skipton, Grassington and Pateley Bridge all on one day in 1766. Meanwhile a local evangelist, Thomas Lee of Haworth, developed a following in Wharfedale and Nidderdale. Conditions in the Dales which must have favoured a non-conformist outlook included a relative remoteness from central authority, fewer omnipotent squires, a growing industrial population of lead-miners and textile-workers and the traditional independence of spirit. Throughout the years of religious turmoil stretching from the Reformation to the emancipation of Catholics early in the nineteenth century, people in the Dales seem to have minimised their differences and only to have indulged in acts of bigotry and persecution when pressured by outsiders.

A sad lapse in this principle occurred in 1752 when the Parson of Pateley Bridge incited the local mob against the Methodist preacher, Thomas Lee. He recalled that he was beaten and rolled in the open sewer, after which,

> my wife and a few friends came up, and the mob seeing her busy about me, some of them said, 'what, are you a Methodist too?', and gave her several blows, which made her bleed at the mouth, and swore they would put her in the river. All this time I lay upon the ground, the mob being uncertain what to do. Some cried out, 'make an end of him', others were for sparing my life; but the dispute was cut short, by their agreeing to put some others in the water. . . .

Lee was placed on a horse and rode the steep hill track to preach a sermon at Greenhow Hill.

During the nineteenth century the building of nonconformist chapels greatly outstripped that of churches, so that the first place of worship which many communities gained was not provided by the established Church. Often funded by a local middle-class worthy, these buildings may seem stark and grey, but their interiors, designed to focus attention on the sermon, may be elegant if not ornate.

Some churches were built during the nineteenth century, though by this time the elements of the local Perpendicular style had been largely forgotten. Features associated with distant corners of England became incorporated into the new churches. An example is the East-Midlands broach spire gracing the attractive hillside church at Birstwith which was built in 1857. A more exotic influence is the Swiss style seen in the tiny church of 1909 at Stalling Busk near Semer Water.

Rebuilding played as important a part as building, for by Victorian times the medieval churches of the Dales were beginning to show their age. Most of the architecture in the church at Aysgarth dates from a restoration in 1865–6.

CHAPTER 7

Drovers and Jaggers, Knitters and t'Owd Man

Industry and trading have long played very important roles in the history of the Dales but because most of the industry arose before the days of factory production the relics are homely and often nestle unsuspected in the rural scene. Several miles of Nidderdale running south-eastward from Pateley Bridge exist as a fossilised industrial region but one suspects that the majority of visitors are quite unaware of this fact. Throughout the Dales many of the cottages and farmsteads were originally the homes of miners, weavers, knitters or quarrymen and this is one region where industry has added greatly to the attractions of the countryside.

The Dales of Yorkshire were closely bound up in the old droving trade. The droving of Scottish cattle for sale in England existed in the Middle Ages but was curtailed by the Anglo-Scottish wars of the fourteenth and fifteenth centuries. It recovered after the union of the Crowns and reached its peak around 1800, when around 100,000 Scottish cattle were driven to English markets each year. But by the 1880s the railways had largely extinguished the 'on the hoof' form of transport. From their pastures in the Highlands and Islands of Scotland the cattle were driven first to markets or 'trysts' in the Scottish Lowlands. Then they were taken in herds of around 200 beasts across the Southern Uplands and along the high tracks of the Pennines, avoiding the areas of settled lowland farming. The herd might be divided into four parts, each one in the charge of a drover and his dogs, and the drovers would cover about a dozen miles before halting at a wayside pasture where a drovers' inn might also be found. Even at the height of the droving trade the Scottish drovers might still wear the traditional plaid and converse in Gaelic, and it is said that when the cattle began to stray they would discard all clothing to pursue them.

The tiny pack-horse bridge at Thornthwaite

Eventually the herd would reach a market in the Dales where dealers from the south and Midlands of England would gather, the cattle being bought and fattened and then resold for slaughter. The most notable market was at Malham. Here Scottish cattle and sheep were sold at a great fair in the Deerpark, between Finkle Street and Deadman Lane. The sale was followed by dancing and formed the main landmark in the year for people from miles around. As the droving trade declined the fair gave way to a local sheep fair held on the village green but this in turn declined. Around 1920 it was reorganised into a series of five autumn sheep and cattle auctions. Many of the old upland droving trails have merged back into the high pastures and moors and the most obvious relic of the old trade is provided by the numerous Drovers' Inns, this being probably the most common pub name in the Dales.

Trade of a different kind was conducted by teams of pack-horses. The trade goods were carried in panniers slung on the sides of the sturdy ponies. These were usually Scottish Galloways or German Jaeger ponies, the latter breed giving rise to the name 'Jagger', which was applied to the man in charge of the team. This unsophisticated form of transport was appropriate in a region where slopes were steep and surfaced roads were few. Around 1800 the jaggers would contract to move cargoes ranging from coal to salt or textiles at a rate of a shilling (5p) per ton for each mile travelled. With the lead horse decked out in bells and ten, twenty or even forty ponies strung

The pack-horse bridge at Yockenthwaite

out in line the teams must have been a colourful sight as they passed across the little arching bridges in the region. The origins of the traffic must go back far into prehistoric times and it was important during the Middle Ages. At the start of the nineteenth century teams of dozens or hundreds of ponies were operating from the northern market towns, but then the improvement of metalled roads and the arrival of the railway brought pack-horse trading to extinction and by the end of the century it was just a memory.

Many of the pack-horse roads were developed by the monasteries to assemble the products of their far-flung estates and to import and distribute vital commodities. Iron, fuel, fish and hides were moved as well as the huge cargoes of wool. Because the sure-footed ponies could negotiate terrain which was closed to wheeled transport the pack-horse roads adopted quite direct lines. In the centuries following the dissolution the traffic on many of the roads increased and bridges were provided or renewed.

Typically the pack-horse bridges span rivers and streams with a single steeply humped arch, so there were no piers to bear the force of floods. Often the bridges were too narrow for use by carts or wagons, while their parapets were kept low so as not to impede the panniers, sacks and square baskets or 'bannisters' carried by the ponies. Such bridges still abound, though several were associated more with farming activities than with long-distant trading.

The most quaint example that I know is near the church at Thornthwaite in Nidderdale, a tiny stone arch standing on an old track from Ilkley to Ripon. A couple of miles away spanning the Nidd between Birstwith and Darley is a much larger and more graceful arch with the partly overgrown traces of a pack-horse road which was used in monastic times approaching it from the north.

While a good measure of building skill was needed to construct an arched bridge, anyone able to call upon a reserve of muscle could build a clapper bridge. These bridges consist of huge flags resting upon crude piers of masonry set on the river bed. Examples of these primitive but not necessarily ancient bridges can be found in the west country and in the Yorkshire Dales. There is one at Linton in Wharfedale and another in Crummack Dale near Austwick.

Compared to the flatter farming countrysides of the English lowlands the Dales was a poor area. The farming population included freeholders, tenants and squatters who had set up cottages and poached land from the commons. Few people could live in comfort from the fruits of farming alone and many had such meagre holdings that even survival was not possible without a secondary occupation. The raw materials for industry abounded in the region in the form of the great annual harvest of fleece. Before the reorganisation of the Yorkshire textile industry on a factory basis, cottage-based textile and spinning industries were found in a multitude of homesteads.

Although many of the old farmsteads still stand, the old textile industries associated with them have vanished without trace. But the importance of the lost industries emerges when one studies the wills and the inventories of the possessions of bygone Dalesfolk. Thomas Atkinson died at Clint in Nidderdale in 1623 and his possessions were listed: they included not only cattle, horses, lambs, swine and fodder but also a stone of hemp and two spinning wheels. John Lewty was a neighbour and died in 1627. His inventory reads as follows:

> 11 cattle; 1 black horse; 7 ewes; and followers; 3 hoggs; 5 hens a goose and goslings; 1 steg [an old gander] 3s 8d; 1 turkey hen; 1 day's work of oats £2 10s 0d; hay and an old scythe 6s 8d; 1 cart body, wheels; 3 pairs of cards [for carding yarn], 8 score herden and samaron yarn [samoran was a cloth of mixed harden or hemp and linen yarns] 12s; 3lbs tow, 2½lbs line, 2lbs coloured yarn 2s; 5¾ yards hersey 15s; 4 yards blue hersey; 1 yard white hersey 10s.

Another neighbour was John Dixon and he died in 1634, leaving the following:

> 4 cows £8 13s 4d; 4 stirks, 1 calf £3 6s 8d; 3 horses £4 10s; 13 sheep £2 10s; hay 10s; 1 cart, 1 loom, 2 pairs great shears for cloth 5s;

1 spinning wheel, 38 lea hemp yarn and some wool 5s 6d; 6 yards hemp cloth, 4 yards linsy, woolsey, 3 quarters white hersey.

Woollen yarns and cloth were not the only textiles produced and John Dixon's inventory mentions hemp cloth or linen. Flax was grown in gardens and small plots in villages like Grassington, and just across the Wharfe from Grassington is Linton, whose Saxon name means 'hemp farm', showing that the hemp industry had a very long history here.

Twelfth- and thirteenth-century relics of the industry can be seen near Newton-in-Bowland in the Forest of Bowland in the form of hemp 'retting' or steeping ponds, where the plant decayed to release the internal fibres, and pondside banks where the hemp was dried. The associated smells and pollution explain why the ponds were dug about 655 feet (200 m) away from the village.

In addition to the widespread weaving and spinning industries there were some localities which specialised in knitting. In the Dent area this craft seems to have developed in Elizabethan times and grew rapidly during the seventeenth century, and within living memory vestiges of it still lingered. The industry was focused on Kendal, whose entrepreneurs farmed out wool to carders, spinners and knitters. The Dent locality specialised in the knitting of stockings and thousands of the soldiers of the eighteenth century marched to war in stockings sold by the knitters of Dent. In the following century oiled yarn or 'bump' was knitted into stockings, jackets or caps. In nearby Sedbergh there was a specialisation in knitting blue woollen caps worn by convicts and good workers were said to complete a dozen caps each day. Men, women and children all knitted at every opportunity and the famous reference by the writer Robert Southey to the 'terrible knitters o' Dent' used the word 'terrible' in its sense as 'formidable' or 'amazing'.

Various attempts were made to establish cotton mills in the Dales, but the Yorkshire air did not suit this Lancashire industry. Mills established at Askrigg, Aysgarth and Gayle in Wensleydale in the 1780s were soon modified to spin woollen knitting yarn. Gayle and villages like Hawes were noted for knitted hosiery while West Burton and Aysgarth were associated with wool combing. The first stages of the Industrial Revolution, which gathered momentum around 1760, were associated with water-powered mills. Nidderdale must have had a more secure flow of water than the limestone dales and acquired a remarkable assemblage of mills. Also its water was softer and more suited to the flax-retting process. Around the middle of the nineteenth century the dale had not only corn-mills and lead-smelters but also mills spinning flax and cotton, weaving linen and silk and making twine. The new mills sucked in local workers who had previously worked on their smallholdings and in cottage wool and linen industries. But the next turn of industrialisation's screw saw the water-

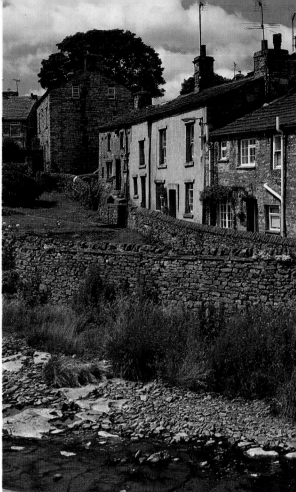

ABOVE LEFT
Ladies at Masham re-create the days of cottage yarn-spinning

ABOVE RIGHT
Lovely Gayle, once a focus of the hand-knitting industry

powered mills closing in the face of competition from large steam-powered factories established close to the fuel supply in the mining areas to the south. As the skies above Leeds, Bradford, Halifax and Huddersfield grew darker and darker, one by one the mill wheels in the Dales ceased to turn.

Writing in his diary at the start of 1897 John Dickinson of Timble in the Washburn valley complained that rural life was declining as the best people migrated to the towns, with the result that 'the hopeful zest and spirit which used to prevail 30 or 40 years ago is dead and life has become little more than a mere idle shuffle'.

Some of the old mills have been demolished, others have been converted into dwellings, and a few have endured in sufficient repair to welcome the modern tourist industry. Towering beside a pub and restaurant just outside Pateley Bridge on the Ramsgill road is the 35-foot (10.6-m) wheel of the former Foster Beck twine and linen yarn spinning mill, this surviving wheel having been installed in 1904. The mill endured until 1966. Further down the dale between Darley and Dacre Banks is Knox Mill, which produced rope and twine and now exists as a restaurant and textiles and furniture store. The mill wheel and the exhibits inside the building recall its former role.

Conditions in the mills could be very hard and workers obliged to leave behind their cottage looms and spinning wheels entered the clattering,

Arkengarthdale; lead-mining once breathed life into this lonely dale

cavernous worlds of factories in which they were expected to work twelve- or thirteen-hour shifts. Some obtained the freedom to work on their smallholdings on Mondays by making up the hours on Friday night. In 1833 the flax-spinning mill at Smelthouses employed seventeen children under the age of thirteen, the three little boys and four little girls who were under the age of ten earning just 1s 6d (7½p) per week, mainly by carrying bobbins to and from the spinning frames.

Though small by comparison with the factories on the coalfields the Dales mills employed up to 150 workers and when they closed the loss of work hit the local communities very hard. When the flax mill at West End in the Washburn valley closed in 1850 the local population was cut by a third; thirty-two cottages in the locality were standing empty in 1951. The community never recovered its vigour and now the hamlet of West End can be glimpsed only after a summer of drought, like that of 1989, when the water of Thruscross reservoir dropped and traces of the old buildings, bridges and tracks emerged.

Lead-mining was no less important than textiles in the history of the Dales. The industry goes back at least to Roman times and was developed by the monasteries; the bumps and hollows of medieval workings are now visible in several places, for example on the slopes above Grassington. The

Venerable Bede in AD 672 mentioned how Swaledale miners met merchants in Catterick to haggle over the sale of their produce. Later monastic overlords, like the Abbots of Fountains and Rievaulx and the Prior of Bridlington, exploited mines. It was the habit for local people and miners to refer to the miner of bygone times as 't'owd man'. Now old men are the only living legacy of an industry which peaked and flourished in the eighteenth and nineteenth centuries. Partly as a result of exhaustion but mainly because of competition from cheap lead imports, the industry declined sharply at the end of the last century. A few workings were reopened during the 1914–18 war but then the lead-mining faded away and one of the toughest of the breeds in a land of tough people began to disappear, departing to mine coal in Lancashire and the north-east.

Lead occurs in the form of lead sulphide or galena in veins injected into the older limestones; the veins also contain other minerals such as fluorspar, zinc, quartz and barytes. There were two main lead-mining regions in the Dales, Swaledale and Arkengarthdale in the north and the Pateley Bridge–Grassington area in the south. Many mining areas have been worked and reworked, with advances in technology changing the nature of operations and with the later endeavours masking the evidence of those that had gone before. Even so it is often possible to recognise primitive efforts to pick along a surface vein or the traces of old circular 'bell pits', the bell-shaped shafts sunk by medieval workers. 'Hushing' was a mining technique with a very long history. A stream was dammed to form a pond and a channel was dug to the vein of lead. Then the dam was breached and the sudden flood scoured away the soil and rubble obscuring the minerals. While a new head of water accumulated the miners loosened the exposed rocks and a grating was placed at the end of the vein. A new flood was released and the heavy galena was trapped by the grating or was dropped by the water before the worthless 'gangue' minerals fell. Much of the bed of the Swale is blanketed in debris from the old hushing grounds. In the seventeenth century German expertise in the cutting of drainage adits allowed shaft mining to exploit veins lying below the water-table and the use of gunpowder for blasting speeded the extraction of lead. Some lead mines in the Pennines had shafts as deep as 400 feet (120 m).

In addition to the mining operations there was valuable employment in the 'dressing' and smelting of ore. The immediate product of mining was 'bouse', a mixture of lead ore and other minerals from the vein. This was all stored in a 'bouse team' or compartment and dressing involved hammering and crushing the ore and then separating out the minerals in a flow of water. The smelting of the ore, essential to free the lead from sulphur, was often accomplished on the fellside close to the mine. Lead has a much lower melting point than other useful metals and this allowed local peat to be used in the smelting if small coal seams could not be found in neighbouring rocks of the Yoredale Series. Flues sealed with turf carried away the noxious gases, some lead condensing from the vapour and being reclaimed.

Until the eighteenth century 't'owd man' was a part-timer who also worked a farm or smallholding. Once the rights to exploit lead belonged to the prospector but after the Norman Conquest mining rights passed to the lords of the manors. Then lords took up to a quarter of the yield of a mine. In the seventeenth century mining companies, like the London Lead Company which was organised by Quakers, were formed and they leased lead-mining rights from the manorial lords. As mining became a more highly capitalised and technological undertaking, t'owd man gradually became a full-time wage-earner. Yet the most that he ever earned was 2s 6d (12½p), paid for a shift of work after 1880.

The old lead industry has left an indelible mark on the countryside and villages of the Dales. This legacy is partly one of ruins, for when lead-mining was in its steepest decline in the decade after 1875 some parishes in Swaledale lost more than two-thirds of their population. Places now apparently redolent of rural life, like Grinton, Muker and Reeth, were in fact devastated by the collapse of industry. In Swaledale above Richmond the population fell from around 7000 to around 2000. Most of the people in Gunnerside village migrated to Lancashire, leaving behind a Methodist church designed for a congregation of 500 and two junior schools, each of which accommodated ninety children. On the slopes around the village and on the flanks of the beck the debris of lead-mining provides a silent testimony to days when the belching chimneys and turning water-wheels proclaimed the vitality of a major industry. Other relics are more subtle, and in desolate Arkengarthdale the inn called the C. B. Hotel is a reminder of the dale's old C. B. Mines, which were bought by Oliver Cromwell's physician, John Bathurst, and then accorded the initials of his son, Charles.

Tumbling chimneys, crumbling bouse teams, the litter and pockmarks of old workings and roofless cottages all add their touches of starkness and pathos to the desolate fells of the lead-working areas. The relics can fascinate, but tread with care for many old shafts and adits have not been made safe.

Yet not all the lead landscapes are scenes of desolation and decay. The rubble and ruins in the nearby countryside suggest that Greenhow Hill hamlet, near Pateley Bridge, had a stake in the lead trade and the pub name 'the Miners Arms' confirms it. Originally the miners lived in hamlets and farmsteads down in the valley and struggled up to work, but following a lawsuit in 1613 it was agreed that cottages would be built close to the mines and the miners would also be provided with plots of ground and rights on the surrounding common. Pastures were also provided for the draught oxen and horses used by the mines. In this way a new settlement was born. After the collapse of the local lead industry it almost died but during the last two decades many of the semi-derelict dwellings have been bought and restored. The experiences of a Yorkshire winter at a height of 1300 feet (395 m) above sea level were presumably not the main attraction.

The old industries made a distinctive contribution to the landscapes of the Dales. The gaunt relics of smelters and mills might disfigure the thinner-blooded countryside of lowland England yet in the robust Pennine areas they usually complement their settings. Industrial failure devastated the population patterns of the Dales and now tourism and recreation are seen as the new employers. But on current evidence and suggested trends one fears that the rural harmony may be shattered by screeching discords.

Chapter 8

Cottage and Farmstead

Any first-time visitor to the Dales is bound to be impressed by the handsome and rugged stone dwellings of the region. Such a visitor will also realise that the traditional or 'vernacular' form of architecture differs greatly from that of other areas. Really to enjoy the building legacy we must learn a little more about it – remembering all the time that the buildings were not created as architectural exhibits, but as homes and workplaces.

If we compare our traditional buildings with those of, say, East Anglia the contrasts are underlined. In the latter region the vernacular materials are not stone but timber framing, mud daub or plaster and hand-made brick. Also, in East Anglia surviving dwellings of the fifteenth and sixteenth centuries are very common but in the Dales they are hardly ever seen and most 'old' buildings belong to the couple of centuries between 1650 and 1850. The reason for the first contrast mentioned is obvious: the shortage of heavy oak timber in the Dales and the abundance of tough stone. The relative youth of most surviving buildings is largely explained by the fact that the revolution which allowed durable homes to be afforded in the south-easterly counties in Tudor times did not reach the north until much later so that here the Great Rebuilding did not gather steam until Georgian times.

The common homesteads built before this time were so poky and rickety that they have vanished, leaving scarcely a trace. Our typical visitor will therefore be amazed to learn that while elegant Regency terraces were being built in the fashionable cities the more humble of the Dalesfolk were dwelling in hovels with thatched roofs supported by pairs of upright curved branches or 'crucks'. Thatch of straw, turf or heather was the traditional roofing material of the Dales, though surviving thatched houses and barns are few and far between and are thoroughly expensive, since thatchers have to be imported from the affluent south.

Around Gunnerside in Swaledale, for example, one can encounter the relics of the old vernacular. The homes of the eighteenth-century lead-miners were cramped and the lower levels of the social spectrum of housing ran from homes let at a rent of £1 per annum to those which commanded rents of £2. These were mainly of a kind known as 'firehouses', with a fireplace at the gable end of the living room which was served by an external chimney. Originally single-storey thatched dwellings, many were improved by removing the thatch, adding new courses of stonework to the walls to make an upper storey and making a new, shallow-pitched roof of stone slabs. Agricultural dwellings were of a plan dating back to the early Middle Ages – and probably back further to the Dark Ages. These 'longhouses' consisted of just two rooms, a living room with an open hearth and a byre for cattle or sheep, often with a 'cross passage' running between the two compartments from front door to back door. Such archaic longhouses do not survive intact but a probable derivative, the 'laithe house', still remains the most numerous kind of farmstead, with thousands of examples from the seventeenth, eighteenth and nineteenth centuries surviving. Here living quarters and byre are separated by a wall, though still standing adjacent, and the dwelling house part has two storeys.

In the old longhouses the crucks, often standing on a low wall, were 'A'-shaped frames formed of curving branches. The width of the dwelling was governed by the length of available timbers but the length of the house could be extended by adding extra frames to create new bays, each bay being bracketed by the cruck frames at either end. Sometimes old documents reveal the length and status of dwellings. Thus in 1635 Anthony Reynard of Clint had a house of no less than seven pairs of posts (six bays) while his neighbour, Robert Marston, had a poky little hovel of only one bay. Marston's holding was worth £1 10s (£1.50) and amounted to little more than an acre (0.4 ha) while Reynard had 25 acres (10 ha) worth more than £15. The records of 1635 also show that both thatch and stone were being used for roofing.

In parts of Nidderdale below Pateley Bridge and in middle Wensleydale a few dwellings built on the medieval cruck-frame principle are still standing and occupied. Unlike the situation in the west midlands, where a similar tradition existed, the pedigree of the old houses in the Dales is not obvious to the passer-by, for the crucks of oak or ash are encased by walls of stone, and roofs in the original thatch style are replaced by those of flag or slate.

The use of local stone has ensured that dwellings in the Dales sit comfortably within their setting. Most villages have a small quarry nearby and quarrying is still an important activity. Modern quarries in the limestone regions, several of which are actually removing the very hills which give the landscape its form, extract pure lime for the chemical industry and rubble for roadstone. In the past there was a limited use of such rubble in building while limestone was burned in little hillside kilns to produce lime both for spreading on the land and for mortar. The mixed rock bands of the Yoredales yielded coal for the kilns and a variety of sandstones, some suitable for rough or regular walling and others which could be split and split again to provide building slates.

Where stones of a modest quality were employed it was necessary to import a tougher grade of stone to form important structural features like lintels, sills and portals. In the Millstone Grit areas, like Upper Nidderdale, entire buildings are made of this robust (and now highly expensive) stone, while the main gritstone quarries exported their wares to other localities. The Scot Gate Ash quarries above Pateley Bridge sent top-quality gritstone far afield, while quarries at Burnsall supplied good lintel- and bridge-making stone to much of Wharfedale; quarries around Muker and Keld served Swaledale in a similar way.

Although there were periods of overlap, the roofing tradition in the Dales had three main phases, represented by thatch of straw, heather or turf; stone flags or false 'slates'; and finally the use of true slates imported by rail from the great nineteenth-century industrial quarries of Cumbria and Wales. Various quarries produced 'thackstones' ('thatch stones') of a fissile sandstone which could be split into narrow slabs, such as the Hill Top quarries in Birkdale in the upper catchment of the Swale or those above West Witton in Wensleydale. The sandstone could not be split into sheets as narrow as those cut from true slates and roofs of thack stones were very heavy. To reduce the weight of the burden to the minimum such roofs were built with the most shallow pitch possible. This was also necessary because it was not practical to secure the stones on roofs steeper than 30°.

The pitch of roofs in the Dales can tell one much about the age and history of the dwellings concerned. Those with very steep pitches were usually the oldest and had originally been thatched, the steep slope of the roof helping the shedding of water from the thatch. Sometimes the ghost of a former gable can be recognised in a gable-end wall, revealing how a single-storey thatched dwelling was converted into a two-storey house roofed in thackstones by raising the side walls and roofing at a shallower pitch. Roofs which are intermediate between the steep thatched type and the shallow thackstone form are usually the youngest and were built to be roofed in imported slates.

One of the most distinctive features of the dwellings of the Dales is the prominent use of 'kneelers', large stones projecting from the ends of the eaves. Originally intended to prevent the coping stones of the sloping gable end slipping down on to unfortunate heads below, kneelers became more decorative features. Those of the seventeenth century or earlier periods are massive with a convex–concave profile but in the eighteenth century more elaborate profiles and mouldings were favoured. In the nineteenth century

the vernacular tradition was abandoned and dwellings became more classical in form, losing the decorative punctuation which had so effectively marked the junction of roof and wall.

The dwellings of the Yorkshire Dales are as often as not the real jewels and focal points in the landscape. Being built of materials which may have travelled less than a mile from quarry to building site they reveal at a glance the character of the local geology. Meanwhile in stone and timber they record the story of post-medieval life in the region. They whisper to us tales of the lead-miner who heightened his single-storey hovel and hoped for better things before retreating defeated to the far-off coalmines, or of the farmer who met his bills and had enough left over to pay a builder to make a roomy laithe house and then used the old longhouse home as a shelter for orphaned lambs. Or perhaps of his Victorian descendant who erected a square and symmetrical farmstead which stands a little apart from the barns and byres arranged around the farmstead. As one Sunday newspaper claims in its slogan, 'All human life is here' – perhaps in the case of the buildings of the Dales the assertion is a little more valid.

One may often regret the details of extensions and alterations but it is fair to say that one can still drive for many miles and see nothing offensive in the local architecture and a great deal that is simply delightful. In the first half of this century population levels were generally static or falling and so there was very little building in tacky brick or rendering. In the second half of this century the demand for building has increased greatly but legislation requiring the use of tolerably harmonious stone has been put in place. At first stone recycled from demolished mills was widely used, but such stone is now hard to find and care will be needed to prevent the use of ugly reconstituted stone or imports like the garish orange ironstone.

A laithe house of 1673 near Greenhow Hill

Flags = Slate roofs.

OPPOSITE ABOVE
The cottages of the Dales echo the rocks of the field walls, stream beds and scars. This is Thwaite in Swaledale

OPPOSITE BELOW
Cottages roofed in local flags by the green at Arncliffe

CHAPTER 9

The Gateways to the Dales

Several towns and townlets claim the title 'the gateway to the Dales'. In reality the region has no single centre and no single gateway. Each contender, however, has its own distinctive character and charm. With its thinly spread population and difficult terrain the region has not been able to generate and sustain its own great urban focus, although within the region small towns and townlets like Settle, Grassington, Pateley Bridge, Middleham and Sedbergh serve as local centres. Then, ranged around the margins of the Dales, either with toeholds in the region or strategically chosen sites at the outlets of the valleys, there are towns like Ripon, Skipton, Harrogate, Knaresborough, Otley and Ilkley, all keen to establish and exploit their links with the upland and valley country.

All these places have interesting histories yet it is ironic that the largest, Harrogate, is very much the youngest. The most historic – in terms of length of service if not of eventfulness – is undoubtedly Ripon. The town stands astride the Skell and close to the Ure, though by this time the anciently sacred river has left the hills and dale behind and the surroundings are partly arable and but gently rolling. Ripon is an excellent base for exploring Wensleydale and Nidderdale and, via the A1, Richmond and Swaledale, while Fountains Abbey is just a few miles away. In the seventh century Ripon emerged as an early ecclesiastical centre associated with St Wilfrid. The staunchest advocates of Ripon's antiquity claim that it was made a self-governing town in 886 by Alfred the Great and was chartered by his grandson Athelstan in 937. If this is the case then Ripon is Britain's oldest chartered town, though less committed experts point out that the forging of charters, freedoms and claims was not unknown to medieval canons like the ones of Ripon, who did receive genuine charters from Henry I and Stephen.

Ripon is dominated by its great minster church. Wilfrid became Abbot of Ripon in 660 and Bishop of York nine years later. His monks built a stone monastic church at Ripon. In the ninth century it was destroyed both by the Danes and by the English King, Eadred. Rebuilt, it was then razed by the Norman armies and its successors were plundered by the Scots and by Parliamentarians. The Saxon crypt of the original church of c. 670 survives beneath the tower of the minster and in medieval times pilgrims queued to see the religious relics which were gathered here. The church displays architecture in the Transitional and Early English style but collapses of the east end and tower and then the rebuilding of the nave at the end of the Middle Ages changed the character of the building – as did the removal of timber spires from the towers in the seventeenth century. In 1836 the minster was redesignated as a cathedral.

The original lay-out of Ripon is still apparent, consisting of the two great foci, the church and the market, and the lane called 'Kirkgate' which links them. The Thursday market continues to be busy and stalls pack the market square, but better known to the tourist is the quaintly garbed hornblower, who sounds his horn nightly at the market cross and in front of the house of the Mayor. This is said to have been done since Saxon times but, as with other aspects of Ripon's history, belief in this is optional. With its early ecclesiastical importance, its market, fertile surroundings and position at the focus of routes approaching the bridging-place on the Ure it is surprising that Ripon did not become a larger town. There was a medieval textiles industry, but this was lost to the towns of the West Riding. There was also a lace-making industry, which finally withered away in the nineteenth century, and there was a medieval spur-making industry, a specialisation shared with the lost village of Clint in Nidderdale.

With its cathedral, old coaching inns and some attractive old shops one might expect that Ripon would be a tourist trap, but it is not. The traffic today is rather more than the centre should be expected to take but, even so, this is one of the author's favourite little market towns.

Knaresborough is Nidderdale's equivalent of Ripon and again the history is a long one. Whereas Ripon's ancient links are with the Church, those of Knaresborough are with the Crown. This was the administrative focus of the great Royal Forest of Knaresborough, whose hunting preserves extended far up the dale and beyond. Early in the twelfth century a castle was built here and dwellings may have been pulled down to create an open market place in the shadow of its walls. The castle was sited to command a dramatic gorge of the Nidd but all that remain are fourteenth-century fragments representing a section of towered curtain wall, parts of the keep and the gatehouse. It was thoroughly slighted by the Parliamentarians after the Civil War.

Knaresborough, the location of England's oldest linen-mill, was once the

OPPOSITE ABOVE
The gorge of the Nidd at Knaresborough

RIGHT
The minster at Ripon

OPPOSITE BELOW
The view from the Cow and Calf rocks above Ilkley

hub of the linen industry and attracted the wares of the cottage industries in the Dales. One Knaresborough character who will have known the linen industry in its heyday was John 'Blind Jack' Metcalf. At the age of six, in 1723, Metcalf was blinded by smallpox, yet he became a noted forest guide and fiddler and, it is argued, left a greater mark on the northern countryside than any other man. He gained some experience of the road-building operations being undertaken in Scotland by General Wade and then set up a haulage business operating wagons between Knaresborough and York. Next he applied his ideas about road-building, which involved the marking of robust but well-drained foundations, to a section of the Knaresborough–Boroughbridge road and then used thousands of bundles of heather to form a firm causeway across the mire between Knaresborough and Harrogate. His reputation spread and in the years which followed he built almost 200 miles (320 km) of road in the northern counties. The only instrument employed to test the quality of the road bed was his strong staff, which he also used to establish levels. In the Dales his work was limited but the lofty Pateley Bridge–Grassington road is of his making. 'Blind Jack' died in 1810, by which time the road-improvement era of which he was a notable pioneer was well established.

Hardly any of Knaresborough's visitors have heard of 'Blind Jack', but many, if not most, are lured by the legend of Mother Shipton, a sixteenth-century seer who inhabited a cave in the gorge. Such prophecies of Mother Shipton as can be said to have come true are loudly proclaimed and the remainder conveniently forgotten. Also close to the Low Bridge is a petrifying spring. Any who find these attractions less than riveting should proceed to the High Bridge, from which the view of the river, the little river boats and the tiers of dwellings perching on narrow shelves on the sides of the gorge is sure to impress.

The outstretched arms of Knaresborough and Harrogate are linked and it was a Knaresborough notable, William Slingsby, who set Harrogate on the path to urban stardom by discovering the mineral springs there in 1571. Products of the peculiarities in the local geology, these springs are either of sulphur (smelling like bad eggs) or of iron, and each type varies according to salinity, the famous chalybeate springs being salt-free iron waters. The springs were discovered on what was described as 'a rude barren Moore' some distance from the straggling little settlement that Harrogate then was. It was probably with some perception that the commentator, Michael Stanhope, wrote in 1626 that 'those that are weak . . . receive more prejudice by the piercing bleake aire, than benefit by the water'.

By this time, however, the reputation of the waters had spread to both poor and rich people, those of 'the best sort' being obliged to fill their cups where the paupers were bathing their sores. As if this were not bad enough, the absence of superior habitations or hostelries in the locality caused difficulties to those of 'the best sort' who were surprised by the efficacy of the purgative qualities of the Harrogate waters. As Stanhope explained: 'What unseemly shifts have I seen many strangers of note put to for want of a convenient place of retirement.' By the end of the century, however, Harrogate was leaving such problems behind and was not only an increasingly popular spa but also a place that people of the best sort would visit to meet others of their class.

From 1840 the Duchy of Lancaster began to invest heavily in the spa. Coal-heated sulphur baths existed and visitors were supplied with barrels of water in their lodgings, but after 1842 the Royal Pump Room was built as public baths and the Royal Baths Assembly Room also survives as a monument to the days when leading members of British society would resort to Harrogate to take the cure. A wealth of hotels and imposing Victorian and Edwardian terraces in blackened gritstone tell a similar tale. After the Second World War the town entered into a decline as ideas in health and recreation changed. Salvation was found in the conference industry and Harrogate now boasts a massive Conference Centre, attitudes to which vary greatly among hoteliers, restaurateurs and retailers on the one hand and local tax-payers on the other. During the great poll-tax furore of

1990 the local politicians attempted to find a private owner for this cash-gobbling cuckoo in their nest.

The discovery and exploitation of the mineral springs provided one important facet of the character of Harrogate. A second was the result of the enclosure or privatisation of the vast and far-flung commons of the Forest of Knaresborough in 1770. The various mineral wells lay scattered in the commons at Harrogate and were a major source of local income. Therefore the unusual step was taken of reserving 200 acres (81 ha) of common as pasture with free access to the public. The legacy of this far-sighted decision is the unique Stray, which consists of broad expanses of lawn which partly surround the old town centre and separate it from the suburbs beyond – a sort of internal green belt.

Harrogate today embodies a strange blend of dowdy grandeur and yuppified vitality, the combination being made more wholesome by the retention of a Yorkshire grittiness and the keen climate from the upland winds which flurry and scurry across the Stray. The town is a good base from which to explore the southern dales of Nidderdale and Wharfedale.

The juxtaposition of an old market town and a spa occurs again in Wharfedale. Otley was an ancient centre of Christianity, and the parish church, which has a Norman north doorway, contains fragments of four Saxon crosses. After the Conquest Otley emerged as the centre of a vast parish and of the estates of the Archbishop of York containing arable land worked by thirty-five ploughs and with no less than sixteen outlying portions or 'berewicks'. The parish extended from the watershed of the Nidd to the banks of the Aire. The original grant to the Archbishop is said to have been made by King Athelstan after the Battle of Brunanburgh in 938, when the Archbishop was established as the head of a great liberty; Henry I confirmed his rights to have his gallows at Otley. The town may have been a market centre since Athelstan's time; a fair was mentioned in 1122 and in 1239 the proceedings were formalised in a charter granting a Monday market and a two-day fair on the vigil and day of St Mary Magdalene (21–22 July).

The market is now much declined from its status as the bustling focus of Wharfedale commerce which it enjoyed from medieval to mid-Victorian times. Memories of the past are evoked by street names like Kirkgate, Westgate, Bondgate and Boroughgate, which incorporate the Viking word for a street, by the narrow lanes and back streets and the old coaching inns. If the urban landscape is less majestic than that of Harrogate or less picturesque than that of Ripon this is compensated for by the fine setting framed by the Wharfe and the 900-foot (274-m) bulk of the hill known by an ancient Celtic name, the Chevin.

Neighbouring Ilkley is not so much evocative of the Middle Ages as of the periods before and after. I have already described how the Roman fort of

OPPOSITE
*The castle (above)
and the Leeds and
Liverpool Canal of
1774 (below) give
Skipton its medieval
and industrial
character*

Olicana on the York–Ribchester road is still outlined by streets in the core of Ilkley, while there is evidence from the geographer Ptolemy that Ilkley was one of nine 'towns' of the Brigantes. After the Roman retreat Ilkley may have been an outpost of the Christian kingdom of Elmet and three fine Saxon crosses from the next Christian era are preserved in the church.

After the Norman Conquest Ilkley became a possession of the Percy dynasty and in 1213 a Wednesday market and a fair of eight days around the day of St Luke the Evangelist (18 October) were gained. Ilkley, however, was overshadowed by its neighbours and drawings from the middle years of the nineteenth century portray a rustic village of thatched dwellings which is unrecognisable in the modern townscape. In the 1840s medicinal springs were developed and hydrotherapy was established. In the later decades of the century Ilkley developed as a spa, smaller but no less refined than Harrogate. Although the spa trade has declined an aura of Victorian and Edwardian gentility still pervades the little town.

The setting of Ilkley is notable, with the profile of the Cow and Calf rocks forming a prominent landmark overlooking the town. On the slopes above it and on Rombalds Moor, which stretches over to Airedale, there are rocks pecked and grooved with the undeciphered 'cup and ring' marks which were chipped into the gritstone boulders by Neolithic or Bronze Age folk. Any stranger to these moors is likely to give vent to a verse or two of 'On Ilkla Moor baht 'at', a dirge which seems to be far better known outside Yorkshire than within it. Luckily, very few singers seem to know more than a couple of verses.

Otley and Ilkley are good bases for the exploration of Wharfedale. Though lying close to the upland and lowland worlds they more plainly mark the meeting of the rural area of the Dales and the industrial arena of the Leeds–Bradford conurbation, lying just to the south of Otley. Not all the relics of factory industry are black and boring and visitors to Otley and Ilkley are urged to venture across Rombalds Moor to Airedale. There they will see the great staircase of canal locks opened in 1774 at Bingley and, nearby, the remarkable industrial townlet built by Sir Titus Salt in the 1850s at Saltaire – the latter currently threatened by new road developments.

Each dale has a long-established town located at a bridging point close to the zone where it broadens and merges into the plain and in Swaledale that town is Richmond. Alan the Red arrived here in 1071 and appreciated the military strength of the rocky river-bluff site. In due course Richmond developed as a town serving the castle above. By 1144 a market charter had been secured and the market and surrounding dwellings came to exist as what was effectively an outer ward of the castle, being enclosed by a town wall which was breached by three main gates. Like the other towns

mentioned, Richmond enjoyed a good economic location near the junction of the contrasting environments of the upland dales and lowlands. During the Middle Ages goods as varied as lead, iron, coal, timber, hides, fish, livestock, wool and cloth were traded there.

Richmond Castle enjoyed a charmed existence. The Scottish raiders generally passed it by, and as the northern threat receded so the town wall was pillaged for building stone. Richmond emerged as one of the most attractive stone-built market towns in England and the seventeenth-century traveller Celia Fiennes found that 'the streets are like rocks themselves'. By Elizabethan times Richmond had established itself as the hub of a local stocking-knitting industry and a survey of this period recorded 'above 100 knytters wch doo make about 166 dozen every weeke'. In 1598 a plague is said to have killed 2200 people in Richmond. However, in 1726 the author, diplomat, spy and convict Daniel Defoe published a third account of his travels, where he wrote:

> Richmond is a large market town. . . . Here you begin to find a manufacture on foot again, and as before, all was clothing, and all the people clothiers, here you see all the people great and small, a knitting; and at Richmond you have a market for woollen or yarn stockings, which they make very coarse and ordinary, and they are sold accordingly; for the smallest sized stockings for children are here sold for 18 pence per dozen [7½p], or three half pence a pair, sometimes less.

The importance of Richmond in the eighteenth century was reflected in the theatre built in 1788. It survived as a theatre for sixty years and then experienced a variety of humbler existences as a granary, warehouse, auction room and billiard saloon. At the start of the 1960s, however, it was refurbished as a Georgian theatre, one of only two such survivals in Britain.

Richmond was also associated with the Swaledale and Arkengarthdale lead industry. During the eighteenth century the lead was carted to a lead yard at Richmond and the carts returned with loads of mining timber. Then the lead was carted to Darlington to be despatched to Newcastle, London or the Continent. In 1846 a branch line from Darlington reached Richmond and the historian of the lead industry, Edward R. Fawcett, recalls how he had 'heard old men relate that they had seen the station goods yard packed with heaps of pig lead awaiting a rise of price in the lead market. When that happy event materialised the whole of the lead was sold and despatched in a few days.'

These then are the towns which sit at the gateways to the Dales. Geographically Skipton is not a gateway of this kind and the dale which it commands, Airedale, is not always perceived as a rural utopia in the way that Swaledale or Wensleydale are. Skipton is, however, a gateway between the verdant worlds of Ribblesdale, Malhamdale and the Forest of Bowland on the one hand and industrial West Yorkshire on the other. As one moves south-eastwards along Airedale, Silsden, Keighley and Bingley signal stages in the transition and at Shipley the continuous sprawl of the Leeds–Bradford conurbation begins. For the proverbial crow the flight from the centre of Skipton to the heart of Bradford is less than 20 miles (34 km), yet but for the Leeds and Liverpool Canal cutting past its core Skipton might seem to be a remote and secluded market town.

Like Richmond and Knaresborough Skipton is emphatically a castle town. Only a gateway remains from the castle built before 1100 by Robert de Romille, the rest being obscured by later castle works. Yet the influence of the Norman castle is plainly etched in the townscape with the market area being formed in a broad street set out to run down from the castle gate. The market is an old one, for some years before 1189 Alice de Romille gave the canons of Bolton the right to trade there free of tolls. In 1203 Skipton also acquired the right to hold an annual fair and in 1597 a livestock fair was gained which took place fortnightly from Easter to Christmas; ten more fairs were won in 1756. Skipton had become both the capital and trading centre of the de Romille's great territory, the Honour of Skipton. The market area still supports markets but it has been reduced in size by the encroachment of flanking buildings. The line of buildings known as 'Middle Row', which forms an island in the High Street, may be another encroachment and it is interesting to see how terraces of dwellings were built to fit into what were formerly the long, narrow garden plots of medieval houses fronting on the High Street.

The pre-Conquest name means 'sheep farm' and this connection was a continuing theme. In 1379 Skipton housed thirteen families engaged in weaving and dealing in cloth as well as thirty-five other families engaged in commerce or crafts and seventy-nine families of labourers. Although Skipton may seem today to be almost quaint, by the seventeenth century its flourishing fair and market made it a place of considerable commercial substance. The dynamic patroness Lady Anne Clifford had the decaying family castle rebuilt in stone in 1655 and the prosperous proprietors of the buildings lining the High Street had these rebuilt in a similar manner. Skipton must then have appeared as a place of considerable elegance and importance. In 1774 the town became connected to the Leeds–Liverpool Canal and Skipton's role as a market town, wool-collecting centre and wool-textile centre was enhanced still further. The new facilities provided by the canal led to the opening of limestone quarries and the burning of lime for mortar and fertiliser.

The stage seemed set for Skipton to develop as a dynamic mill town importing coal by barge and specialising in worsted and cotton. To some extent this promise was fulfilled during the nineteenth century, yet Skipton

OPPOSITE ABOVE
*The Folly in Settle of
1679*

LEFT
*The Pateley Bridge
show is one of the
greatest in the Dales*

failed to erupt into a Leeds or even into a Dewsbury. There are industrial areas around the canal but the barges there are associated with the tourist trade and the atmosphere in the parts of the town which visitors explore is that of the timeless market centre. Whatever the chamber of commerce may have lost on the swings of industry it has gained on the roundabouts of trade – and the newest shopping arcade here shows modern architectural design in uncommonly good taste. Skipton is a good base for exploring the south-western area of the Dales and a favoured stopping place for traffic bound from south-eastern England to the Lake District.

Further along the much used and abused A65T is Settle, one of the very few places of any size to lie deep within the Dales. Settle certainly bustles, but most of the traffic is going through rather than to. Like other towns and townlets in the Dales, Settle has deep historical roots. Though there was no great church or castle the origins go back to a market charter granted to Henry de Percy by Henry III in 1248 and the Tuesday market still endures.

OPPOSITE BELOW
*The sheep fair at
Masham*

The little townscape is not medieval but the product of the seventeenth, eighteenth and nineteenth centuries and although Settle has not won many headlines in the history books it has acquired a fascinating architectural legacy, ranging from the vernacular to the curious. The old lay-out seems to be of a trio of roads converging on the market place yet old Settle was not as homogeneous as this and Upper Settle or Over Settle in the east was once distinct. This area has a remarkable building which is known now as the Folly but originally as Tanner House, and it was built by one Thomas Preston in 1679. Most houses are status symbols as well as homes but here the quest for grandeur exceeded the resources of owners, whose wealth was all invested in the ornate façade. The impact of the display of windows is maximised by carrying the surrounds right into the corners of the home. More interesting architecture is seen in the Shambles of almost the same date on the northern side of the market. The cottages here had their living quarters placed above an arcade and some of the quaintness disperses when one learns that the ground-floor levels served as butchers' slaughterhouses. The cottages gained an upper storey in the nineteenth century. Strangers may know Settle best for its association with the controversial Settle–Carlisle railway. Although the famous Ribblehead viaduct is some distance away Settle has its own railway viaduct, built during the 1870s. In the decades which followed, a small population of paupers lived in hovels in the shelter of the arches of the viaduct.

Moving down the urban scale we come to Masham in Wensleydale, a townlet organised around a vast market place which tells of former commercial glories. It was in 1393 that Stephen le Scrope granted a Wednesday market and two annual fairs to Masham, but life here must have had a longer history than this for the large church of St Mary is a partly Norman building and a Saxon cross stands close beside it. The commerce of Masham was related to the place's role as a bridging point on the Ure. We do not know when the first bridge was built but it must have been of wood. In the middle of the sixteenth century the quarter sessions at Thirsk ordered that the county should raise £400 to repair a timber bridge at Masham. In 1732 there was a great flood on the Ure, which swept away both the bridge at Masham and another not far away at Tanfield. The authorities, perhaps tiring of replacing timber bridges, then erected a fine stone bridge of four arches in 1755.

Memories of the old commerce of the area are stimulated by the road to Grewelthorpe named Badger Lane, not with reference to the animal but to the small traders known as 'badgers' who were licensed to deal in corn. A picture of the activities of Victorian Masham can be gained from the records of 1851, which reveal three straw-bonnet makers, some eleven blacksmiths, seventeen dressmakers, fifteen shoemakers, fifty-one farm workers and a remarkable fifty-eight domestic servants. Not all the colourful traders have gone, for modern Masham has the workshops of both a potter and a glassblower.

Masham is a place of considerable charm and is far less distorted by tourism than some towns and villages with less interest to offer. Saturday visitors find a market which is merely a shadow of its former self – yet there are still the fairs. Masham is the only townlet in the Dales to have given its name to a type of sheep – the noble crossbred ewe with the distinctive crinkly fleece. A series of sheep sales and fairs are held here at the start of autumn at which both local and exotic breeds are represented – and they are real fairs, not media and tourist events. Prices for the local stock can be quite high since southern gentlemen farmers like to boast of having bought their Masham ewes at Masham. There may be no better place to see northern hill farmers doing what they most like to do – talking and haggling over sheep.

Pateley Bridge lies deep in Nidderdale at a bridging place where the old monastic route from Fountains Abbey to Grassington and Kilnsey crosses the old valley route proceeding up the dale and thence to Masham in Wensleydale via Lofthouse. It also forms a link between the former industrial villages and hamlets of the middle dale and the seemingly remote countrysides of the upper dale. The place-name refers to the 'pate' or badger and just across the river is Bewerley, a name associated with the beaver, showing how wild this area may have been in Saxon times. Pateley gained a market early in the fourteenth century and since then it has had a varied history. It probably did not amount to very much in medieval times, for early in the seventeenth century Pateley was said to consist only of sixteen to twenty dwellings. Until the nineteenth century it was a focus for the local flax and linen industry, while the association with lead-mining goes back at least to Roman times. At the end of the eighteenth century the market was still flourishing and in 1794 the Board of Agriculture surveyors reported that Pateley was 'a fine thriving place'. In addition to the town's butchering and linen industries they mentioned the export of salted butter and hams to London (the meat being too lean for the Lancashire trade) and the sale of hogs fattened on oatmeal to the Lancashire mill towns. Within a few decades, however, the market was in decline and Pateley was finding salvation in lead-mining and quarrying.

Had a scheme of 1820 come to fruition Pateley and Knaresborough would have shared the first public railway in England, which was planned to handle quarrying and flax/linen products. It was not until 1849 that parliamentary approval was gained for a Nidderdale line to Pateley Bridge and not until 1860 that work began. It was completed in 1862 at a cost of £8000 per mile. Then, between 1904 and 1908, a light railway was built from Pateley to the head of the dale at Angram, where two reservoirs were being built. With the completion of Scar House reservoir in 1936 the light railway was demolished, while the Nidd Valley line closed to passengers in 1951 and to goods in 1964.

These railways opened Nidderdale to the first trickles of tourism, but there can be no doubt that were they to exist today then Pateley would be a major centre of tourism in the Dales. As it is, the town is a local shopping and recreational centre which still just manages to avoid being twee. The core of the town consists of a straight and narrow sloping High Street lined by shops, some of which are now of much more interest to visitors than to locals. But nobody could deny the picturesque quality of the scene.

The townlet is noted for its remarkable summer displays of hanging baskets, and after the threat of frost recedes at the start of June the proprietors vie to produce the finest floral displays. The most evocative feature of Pateley, however, is missed by most visitors and consists of the ruins of the Church of St Mary sited high above the townlet. A chapel was established here before 1321 and from the ruins of the medieval church one has a fine view of the valley, Pateley and the replacement of St Mary's. Pateley folk were far too canny not to take advantage of a grant made available in 1818 for the building of new churches in parishes with more than 4000 inhabitants but church space for less than 1000. All who have made the steep uphill slog from Pateley to St Mary's will understand why the decision was taken to build anew rather than to repair and enlarge the old church. The more accessible Church of St Cuthbert's was completed in 1826.

There are other places which hover in the marchlands between the village and the town: Hawes, Grassington and Leyburn, for example, and all are explored in the chapter on the individual dales in Part Five. Everyone will agree that the region is approached via some highly attractive and inviting gateways; these gateways tend to face south and east rather than north and west, a fact largely explained by the south-eastward alignment of the great valley corridors.

PART THREE

Bishop Auckland
Gateway to
Weardale

CHAPTER 10

The Ways of the Weather

People holidaying abroad in the more popular resorts tend to encounter weather which is mainly sunny but wet from time to time. Between these two extremes there is not a lot to talk about – one sunny day is very much like another. In the Dales, however, the weather has infinite nuances and the subtlety of the light is such that a scene may never be seen twice in quite the same way. Most visitors come in July and August. These are the months when the weather is warmest, but they are also those when the personality of the region is least strongly stated. There will be many locals, like myself, who prefer May and October, while the scenes which follow a hard January snowfall are unforgettable.

Experts make a distinction between weather – the day-to-day changes in conditions – and climate – the broad annual pattern of warmth and wetness. The pattern of weather in the Dales is one of great variability and that of climate is of cool, moist winters and summers which are mild, if late in getting going. Generalisations about such things are, however, doomed to failure because of the enormous variations from place to place. Altitude, exposure to winds from this quarter or that and aspect (whether the site faces north, south, east or west) each has an enormous effect and over the centuries man has tailored his activities to take account of these things.

Most recently complications have arisen not only from the natural changes in climate, which have brought a shift from the conditions prevailing at the start of this century when skating on the frozen Wharfe at Otley was a winter recreation, but also from the 'greenhouse effect' which seems to be creating warm, wet winters with storm-force winds of exceptional violence.

In the Dales, as in other parts of England, most of the weather comes from the west, borne on westerly winds blowing above the warm waters of the Atlantic. The further east one moves in the Dales the further one is from the moderating influence of the Atlantic, so the more the climate tends to be cool in winter and warm in summer. Rain and snow clouds are borne on the westerlies and much of their load of moisture is shed as they rise over the western summits and plateaux of the Pennines. Thus the west of the region is much wetter than the east and the high ground is wetter than the low. The rain-lashed fells in the north-west of the region receive around 60 inches (1500 mm) of rain and snow each year – comparable to the amounts received in the Lake District – while places in the east of the Dales may receive only 25 inches (650 mm), similar to the pattern in Kent. At Hawes in Upper Wensleydale around 60 inches of rain fall each year, while the middle section of Nidderdale receives about 40 inches (1000 mm).

The effect of altitude on the climate of the Dales is enormous. On the high plateaux of the Pennines plant communities left over from the Ice Ages still linger and above Teesdale, to the north-east of our region, reindeer moss lichen can still be found. Yet at the junction of the Dales and the Vale of York the climate is little different from that of the Chilterns or Cotswolds. In these topsy-turvy times of the greenhouse effect it is hard to describe current climate, and snowfall over much of the region has tended to be lighter in recent years. On the most lofty and exposed of the north-western fells snow may lie for a third or more of the year. Blizzards cause their own particular problem, especially if they are unexpected, obliging farmers to dig out sheep which get caught on the high fells.

Of more permanent concern to the farmer is the length of the period in the year when the daily average temperature is above 42°F (8°C). This, in effect, is the growing season when grass grazed by stock is naturally replenished. In the most lofty and inhospitable places the growing season lasts for a mere one-third of the year, but down in the valleys where the roads and the tourists go the growing season is almost everywhere longer than 200 days. The shorter the growing season the more the farmer needs his store of winter fodder, but the less are the opportunities to grow it.

An important zone in the landscape of the Dales is marked by the 1000-foot (305-m) contour line. Above this line the conditions are usually too unfavourable to permit the cultivation of arable crops and though some hay is grown above this height the emphasis falls upon the production of sheep and cattle. There were times when it was September before the highest hay crops were ready for harvest, but the modern fashion for silage-making removes the need for warm sunlight to dry the cut hay crop.

Strangers exploring the region may wonder why farmsteads stand high on the hillsides on exposed plateaux with nothing but a row of wind-bent trees to protect them from the blast, while there are few if any dwellings in the secluded haven of the valley bottom. In former times valley bottoms were

Snow in Swaledale. Most of the livestock have been sold or are sheltered in barns but any sheep on the fells are unable to graze

badly drained and marshy while rivers were unregulated and highly prone to flood. It was best to have one's feet well out of the water. Many villages in the Dales stand not on the river flood plain but on old river terraces a few precious feet above the plain, the terraces being relics of a former and slightly higher flood plain. A homestead sited in the depths of a valley might seem delightfully secluded in summer, yet in winter it might never see the sun at all. Also, cold dense air rolling down steep valley slopes will tend to settle in 'frost hollows' on low ground, where the microclimate is exceptionally cold.

The north-west to south-east orientation of the main dales produces a situation where the valleys have one slope facing to the north-east and one facing to the south-west. In both agricultural and psychological terms, the south-facing slope, which receives far more sunlight than its neighbours, is greatly favoured. Farmers are well aware of the importance of aspect, but one wonders how many home-buyers take it into account when house-hunting in the balmy days of summer.

The farmer in the Dales must have an intimate knowledge of the details and vagaries of the local climate. Although hay may be the only crop grown he or she is no less a servant of the seasons than the lowland farmer growing wheat or vegetables. He or she must know when heavy snowfalls threaten so that flocks can be driven down from the hills to more secluded pastures, know when to provide the lambing flock with an 'early bite' of the grass which has come into growth on the lowland grazings and when to remove the stock from meadows where the winter fodder crop will be grown. The farmer must also understand the degrees to which different breeds and crossbreeds are hardy, for those types which are most productive of meat or wool tend to be least resistant to the rigours of the hill climates. He or she also needs to know the poorly drained pastures likely to cause foot rot in a flock and the grazings which are deficient in one or other of the essential minerals. Only by gaining this close understanding of the farm environment can the hill or valley farmers hope to survive and prosper. In the past tradition, which embodied the accumulated experience of generations, was the guiding light. Now, however, the pace of change undermines the dictates of tradition. Agricultural policies change so that the dairyman may need to learn the craft of the shepherd; new breeds and crossbreeds displace the familiar livestock, while shifts in the climate itself present a whole new range of opportunities and perils.

CHAPTER 11

The Farming Seasons

Farming moulded the landscapes of the Dales and here there are no suitcase farmers or barley barons who can sow a crop and then sit back while the subsidies roll in. Farming life is locked into a 'round of the year', an annual cycle of life in the course of which the scarcely perceptible shifts in warmth, length of daylight, moisture and sunlight provide the essential landmarks in the calendar of toil. We can explore such cycles of activity and seek to understand the meaning of the field compartments of the working countryside. But, first, it is as well to recognise what we see within these fields: the farm animals of the Dales.

Farming patterns change as one moves from the broad river plains, through the steep-sided valleys to the grazings of the high fells. In the relatively lush lowlands the emphasis has been on dairy farming and a holding of around 300 acres (120 ha) can provide a very decent living. In the valleys each farm tends to span a range of environments and various kinds of mixed farming involving beef cattle and sheep are found. On the sparse grazings of the fells a hill farm of 3000 acres (1214 ha) may be needed to support a family, and sheep are the main source of income, although beef herds may sometimes be grazed because the cattle will take the coarser grasses which the sheep have rejected.

Little grain is grown in the Dales; both the cool moistness of the climate and the rugged terrain militate against such efforts. There is, however, plenty of evidence of arable farming in the former centuries when starvation and self-sufficiency were features of local life. Grain was even sown in Teesdale, to the north of the Yorkshire Dales, during the years of the Little Ice Age and notes found in an old family Bible reveal oats being reaped in a snow-covered field in 1782 and corn (wheat?) being cut during a hard frost on 10 November 1799.

The livestock of the Dales vary from one farming environment to another and they have also varied through time. These changes are partly caused by fashions in consumer taste. A century ago pigs weighing 40 stone (254 kg) were reared to be butchered and salted for sale at Otley market, while currently there is talk of introducing little Welsh sheep to the Dales to produce small saddle of lamb cuts to be served in fashionable restaurants. In quite distant times the cattle of the Dales were longhorns, a breed long in horn and body and now likely to be seen only in parks or some 'western' movies. During the eighteenth century some of the larger landowners experimented in the selective breeding of a new strain, the shorthorn. In 1822 it was possible to produce a register of the breed, and a century or so later distinct beef and dairy strains had been developed. The shorthorn now became the typical cattle of the Dales, stocky beasts seen in a variety of colours: white and mottled patterns of red and white, and blue and white.

As a boy in the Dales in the 1950s I can recall three leading types of cattle, the shorthorn, the Friesian and the stately brown and white Ayrshire. The large Ayrshire dairy cattle are seldom seen today and the distinctive black and white Friesians have enjoyed enormous popularity at the expense of the dairy shorthorn. It was only in 1904 that a British Friesian Society was formed, yet now these cattle seem to be a timeless and essential component of the plain and valley scenes. An advantage of the Friesian is its versatility, for while mainly a dairy breed it can be raised for beef, and ageing milk cows are acceptable to butchers. Among other native breeds of cattle which could be seen in the Dales were the hardy and unmistakable Highland cattle and another hardy Scottish breed, the dense-coated black Galloway, sometimes mated with a white shorthorn bull to produce robust blue beef calves well adapted to the high pastures. Today the more traditional types of native cattle can still be seen but it is becoming increasingly difficult to identify the parentage of most animals. Foreign types, notably the Charolais and the Simmental, have been introduced into the breeding pool in efforts to produce leaner or more rapidly maturing cattle and the offspring from these crosses, sometimes white or dusty-coloured, may not be easily recognised.

The Yorkshire Dales is a region with a long tradition of sheep-farming. Early in the Middle Ages the various monastic houses created their empires of sheep runs. The vastness of the ranges allowed sheep to be moved from grazing to grazing, thus preventing the build-up of diseases in particular pastures, while the monks became expert in the treatment of ailments. After the decline and then the dissolution of the monasteries their empires were sold to private speculators, fragmented and tenanted, and in due course efforts were made to improve the quality of the stock.

The most basic distinction in sheep-farming today is between the wiry, hardy breeds kept by hill farmers to graze the impoverished upland pastures and the heavier and more productive sheep raised on the richer grazings of

Friesians, like these at
Pinker's Pond in
Wensleydale, have
become the
characteristic cattle of
the Dales. Penhill
forms the backdrop

the valleys and plains. The two forms of farming are closely linked, the rugged sheep of the uplands being crossed with lowland rams or 'tups' to produce the stock seen in the valleys.

The three main types of sheep seen on the fells are the Swaledale, the Dalesbred and the rough fell. In all these hill breeds both ewes and rams are horned. The rough fell breed is most likely to be seen where the Pennines approach the Lake District; the fleece is long and does not curl and the sheep has a large area of white on its face. Most visitors will have difficulty in distinguishing between the Swaledale and Dalesbred breeds, though the form of the white face-markings can provide some clues: the Swaledale often seems to have dipped its nose in a bucket of milk, while the face of the Dalesbred has two white patches. The Swaledale is a very old breed which embodies centuries of acquired adaptation to the rigours of life on the northern fells. The Dalesbred is a newer strain derived from crosses between two of Britain's hardiest sheep, the Swaledale and the Scottish black-face. It now breeds true to type and is a recognised breed in its own right. All these upland sheep are sure-footed and protected by dense, weatherproof fleeces which produce a good length of wool or 'staple'. However, the wool is coarse and is used mainly in the carpet industry.

The sheep-farmers of the valleys seek to marry the hardy qualities of the hill sheep with the higher yields of mutton and wool associated with the lowland breeds. To achieve this, ewes of the various fell breeds may be crossed with the tup of the Wensleydale or Teeswater breeds. These are large, handsome sheep similar in appearance and recognised by their tightly curled fleece. The results of such crosses – Dalesbred × Teeswater, Swaledale × Wensleydale and so on – are halfbred sheep known as Mashams. They are attractive sheep, taller and of a heavier build than the hill breeds, with a fleece which hangs in crinkly ringlets and black and white markings on their faces and legs. Alternatively, the Swaledale ewe may be crossed with a Leicester tup. Though popular with some hill farmers the Leicester struggles to survive in the harsh upland conditions, there being, so farmers say, 'nothing so ready to meet its Maker'. This cross produces a halfbred lamb known as a 'mule' or 'greyface', such types often being recognised by the convex, rather Roman profile to the face, inherited from the father. A quite different type of halfbred ewe which is gaining some popularity results from a cross between a Cheviot ewe and a Border Leicester tup. The offspring are white-faced and, to my eyes, are ungainly sheep reminiscent of white bull terriers. Traditionally sheep farmers have made their profit from the ewes which have raised twins or triplets. These crossbreed ewes, however, are said to be poor mothers which seldom have more than one lamb but their lambs put on weight very rapidly to offset the poorer aspects of the cross.

Some Mashams and mules are sold out of the Dales for fattening, others are kept by valley farmers. All adult Mashams are ewes, the males being sent to market as lambs. Farmers keeping a breeding flock of Masham ewes will then cross them with a lowland tup to produce lambs for sale at market (and will, of course, also shear the Mashams and sell the wool). The most popular cross is with a Suffolk tup, a chunky animal with unmarked black face and legs.

In the spring and summer fields and on the fells of the uplands the visitor will see flocks of Dalesbred, Swaledale or rough fell ewes with lambs of a similar type, raised to perpetuate the breed, or else with halfbred lambs of the Masham or the mule type. Meanwhile, in the valleys Masham or mule ewes will be seen with crossbred lambs which often have black faces inherited from a Suffolk father. In recent years there has been much experimenting, and the crossing of Masham and mules with a variety of breeds of tup has produced a lamb population of a highly varied appearance.

Working dogs are indispensable on the upland sheep farms. Records from Victorian times suggest that a variety of dogs were employed, some being rough, tan, retriever-like animals. Now the use of rough-haired Border collies is virtually universal and the breed combines the highest levels of stamina and intelligence. It was probably introduced by the old Scottish cattle-drovers. The shepherd exploits but controls the dog's hunting instinct. It will readily chase sheep but careful training is needed to teach it to drive sheep towards or – and this is far more difficult – away from its master or 'pack leader'. The best dogs can anticipate the shepherd's intentions and work independently of him when screened from view. In addition to brains, speed and endurance the shepherd wants a brave dog that will face up to a stubborn tup or a ewe guarding her lambs. He also seeks a dog with self-control that will not stampede a flock or snap too sharply at the heels of sheep. Less easy to explain is the way a dog 'eyes' a flock – a dog which has a 'hard eye' tends to concentrate too strongly on a small number of sheep. As well as exploiting the dog's natural instincts to hunt and to regard its owner as the dominant pack leader the shepherd can also exploit the herd instincts of the sheep, which run together for safety. This makes it possible to move a large flock, but then individuals are rather harder to isolate. The dogs are taught to respond to a code of whistles or to verbal commands: 'come by' meaning 'go right' and 'way here' meaning 'go left'.

Sheep-dog puppies are delightful and television programmes about sheep-dog trials have increased the fame of the breed. Border collies, however, are quite unsuitable as pets in the typical household. They are working dogs bred to run for as long as the day is long. The author's crossbred collie has one long and two shorter walks each day and fairly constant company. Such active and intelligent dogs need this attention and exercise, and if bored and neglected they will soon find trouble, their innate drives leading them to chase sheep or vehicles.

ABOVE Good Swaledale sheep; both sexes of the breed carry horns

OPPOSITE A mixed flock of hardy sheep on the old common above Grassington. Swaledale, Dalesbred and Jacob types are among the flock members

BELOW Masham ewes and lambs: note the large stature and the long, crinkly fleece

Some dogs are callously shot at the end of their working lives, others become the pets that they were never allowed to be while at work. Most hill farmers will talk long and with great authority about their qualities, the champion trial dogs exchanging hands for four-figure sums. The sheep-dog trials at the summer and autumn shows allow the shepherds to display the talents of their dogs, almost all of which leave the glamour of the trial ring for day-to-day work on the fells.

In the Dales hill, valley and plain play complementary roles in the raising of sheep, and the same is true in the farming of cattle. The limestone pastures of the fells are rich in calcium, which encourages the formation of strong bones, but the grass is relatively sparse and its growing season is short. Some upland farms keep herds of 'store' cattle. These are cattle which are grazed in the uplands during the seasons when the pastures are in growth and which are auctioned to lowland farmers during the autumn for wintering on the lusher lowland pastures and fattening on winter fodder crops. Lowland cattle are also grazed in the uplands during summer, allowing winter fodder crops to be grown by their owners on land which they have vacated.

There is also a close relationship between the beef and dairy cattle trades. Dairy cows – almost invariably Friesians – must calf each year to maintain the milk supply. The best of the female or 'heifer' calves are kept to maintain the herd and the remainder of the calves are sent to market. Alternatively, the farm may have a 'flying herd'. In such cases any replacements to the dairy herd are bought in as pedigree Friesians and the cows in each herd are crossed with a bull of a beef breed, perhaps a Charolais or an Aberdeen Angus, to produce beef calves which are destined for fattening by an upland rearer of store cattle.

In recent years dairying has declined in the more remote parts of the dales and is becoming concentrated on the larger lowland and valley farms which can support huge and highly automated milking parlours. The days when an upland farmer might keep a dozen or fewer dairy shorthorn cattle are fast disappearing. The once-familiar sight of a couple of milk churns waiting at the roadside for collection is seldom seen and now chilled milk is collected by large tankers which have difficulty in negotiating the narrow tracks of the Pennines. Local cheesemaking has declined almost to extinction and recently EEC quota arrangements designed to reduce the milk and butter 'mountains' have hit the small producer very hard and signalled a switch to sheep production.

Though words like bull, calf, ewe and lamb are universal, a special vocabulary is needed to converse with a Dales farmer and the following words will prove useful:

stirk: all cattle between one and two years old

steer: a bullock

heifer: a young cow until birth of her second calf

gimmer hogg: a female sheep between being a lamb and being a ewe, that is,
   between the age of six months and first shearing or lambing

hogg: a sheep of any sex between lamb stage and shearing

shot lamb: a weakling

two-tooth sheep: a one- or two-year-old sheep

four-tooth sheep: a two- or three-year-old sheep

tup: a ram

wether: a neutered male sheep

Since the hunters and fishermen of the Middle Stone Age first penetrated the Dales a seasonal rhythm has governed the affairs of Dalesfolk. Stone Age hunters emerged from the valleys in summer to hunt the deer on the high plateaux, Bronze Age herdsmen drove their cattle up to the summer grazings on the fells and the spread of farming intensified the reliance on the subtle changes which bring grass into growth and cause seeds to germinate. In monastic times lambing ewes in flocks of about 200 members were brought down from the upland grazings, with protected shelter being provided in special sheep houses. Here, as today, the ewes were fed on hay harvested from nearby meadows but unlike the modern situation the ewes were milked and the milk converted into cheese and butter. Sometimes goats were kept to provide milk for the lambs.

Farming in the Dales is mainly about growing grass and this is governed by the changing seasons. The old farmers have a saying that hay in the barn is money in the bank. The conditions vary greatly from the sheltered valleys to the windswept fells, even if the two environments are less than a mile apart. We can compare the annual cycles on the valley and upland sheep farms. Firstly, let us look at a real farm in the middle-valley section of the Nidd. Here the grazing is excellent, needing only a little lime, but with an area of only 38 acres (15 ha) it would scarcely support the farming family if they did not have additional employment. The good pastures sustain a permanent flock of 100 ewes, three tups and, in spring and summer, about 200 lambs.

A few lambs are born in the second week of January but the main lambing is timed to coincide with the regrowth of the grass and runs from the second week in March to the second week in April. The fields are sufficiently sheltered to allow lambing to take place away from the farmstead but weaklings, their mothers and orphans are reared in a barn for special attention and protection from foxes and dogs. Ewes cannot manage more than two lambs without suffering to some degree, so the flock of 'pet lambs' kept around the farm is largely composed of members from sets of triplets which have been removed for human rearing. At the start of May the sheep and lambs are removed from the hayfield and in July or August

*A Swaledale flock
wintering in valley
pastures near Linton;
the background slopes
are terraced by
medieval strip lynchets*

the hay crop is cut and dried in the sun. High summer is also the time when the sheep are sheared and dipped, the fleece providing a secondary source of income. The main shearing work is done by members of a peripatetic shearing gang though the best sheep are sheared by the shepherdess. Grass dried in the hay meadow is used as winter feed for ewes prior to lambing, but though it is extremely nutritious they still prefer grass. In September the lambs are sent to market and the farming cycle begins again. In the course of their brief lives the lambs have received no artificial food and have eaten only grass, the region's great resource.

On this farm various experiments are being carried out to improve the quality of the lambs. The main flock consists of Masham ewes but four tups have been employed in crosses, the 'conventional' Suffolk, a Shropshire and two French breeds, a Rouge de l'Ouest and a Vendeem. The Shropshire cross did not prove successful but the other three appear to be good. In addition to the Masham, a small flock of Derbyshire gritstone ewes has recently been acquired. These medium-sized sheep with pronounced black and white patches on their faces do not look exceptionally rugged yet they are known to flourish on the meanest grazings and have a modest grass

*A Border collie
waiting to compete at
sheep-dog trials*

intake on the good pastures. They also produce a heavier fleece than the Masham and it is hoped that the Gritstone-Rouge cross will prove a good one since it has received expert acclaim.

The life of a sheep farmer is quite different from that of the wealthy southern barley baron. Sheep are not as robust as they appear to be and flocks must be constantly scrutinised for signs of foot rot, mineral deficiency or the various diseases which may suddenly erupt. Stray dogs are a perpetual menace, while at night there is the threat from the organised bands of rustlers which plague the Dales. There is no season of rest.

On the hill farms the season of activity which begins with the growth of new grass is much shorter and a far larger farm is needed to support a family. The average farm will produce about 300 lambs for sale each year and family income depends upon the level of prices at the autumn sales and the numbers of twins and triplets produced. The old system of calculating the number of sheep that a hill farm could support was to divide the acreage by three and multiply it by two. This shows the contrast in conditions with the valley farm which can support about three large and relatively greedy Masham ewes to the acre.

Lambing is usually delayed until April, the ewes having been served in November. During the lambing season the ewes are brought to the most sheltered pastures and paddocks near the farmstead. By this time the most serious threat of snow has passed but in the preceding months snow poses a severe challenge, not so much in terms of the loss of ewes buried by snowdrifts which cover the walls under which they have sheltered but from the blanketing of the vegetation on which they depend.

The hill farmer will produce Masham ewes for sale to the valley and lowland farmers and also Swaledale or Dalesbred ewes to renew his breeding flock. Ewes of four or more years old may also be sold to the lowlands while the 'wether' lambs too are sold for fattening on the richer lowland pastures. The shortness of the growing season and the poverty of the pastures has resulted in the provision of subsidies which are invested in winter food supplies so that the flocks which are seen on the fells in summer can survive the lean, dark days of winter.

Drystone walls endow the landscapes of the Dales with an invaluable facet of their distinctive character. Though a greatly loved part of the scene they were not built to grace the countryside but to serve crucial practical purposes. As well as serving to mark the boundaries between particular properties they also reflect the seasonal rhythms of farming. They helped to keep stock out of the meadows where hay was growing or to protect crops of oats and barley, and after the harvest stock could be penned in these fields to feed on the autumn grass or graze the stubble. Then, as winter tightened its grip, the flock of lambing ewes could be driven down to walled paddocks close to the farmstead and fed with hay until the close of the lambing season.

In the Dales one will see field walls of many different ages. On the fells above Grassington and in several other places there are tumbled but quite recognisable drystone walls of limestone boulders which date from the Iron Age. Other walls were built by the monks and by those who took over their lands, but the greatest age of wall-building took place in the eighteenth and early nineteenth centuries. To the west of Burnt Yates village in Nidderdale there survives a long stretch of the boundary wall of the Fountains Abbey estate. It is known locally as 'Monk Wall'. The village stood close to a gate in the wall and its name probably describes a gate that had been burned. In monastic times the countryside was much more open. The fields tilled by the peasants were protected by living hedges or by hurdles of woven branches which could be removed to allow beasts to graze the stubble. Some walls were built in medieval times, often replacing hedgerows, and sometimes they survive; medieval walls tend to be less regular than those of later centuries and frequently include large, angular boulders in their bases.

More evident than the legacy of medieval walls are the traces of cultivation. Visitors to the Dales during a snowmelt will pass through countrysides striped green and white. The patterns are a legacy of ridge and furrow ploughing and snow lingers in the furrows between the old plough ridges. The medieval peasant farmers deliberately created these long, slightly curving ridges in the ploughsoil, probably to assist the drainage and so that crops would survive in the intervening furrows during drought and on the ridges when the fields were saturated. A strip consisted of a bundle of one to half a dozen or more ridges and the peasant tenant might hold fifteen to thirty strips scattered across the vast arable fields, each strip being around an acre (0.4 ha) in area.

Far more dramatic than the traces of medieval strip farming are the staircases of plough terraces or 'strip lynchets' which pleat the valley sides in parts of Wharfedale, Wensleydale and Swaledale. Strip lynchets survive in other parts of England but in the Dales they are known locally as 'raines'. Sometimes mistakenly described as Roman vineyards, these terraces appear to have been carved into the slopes in the hungry years before the Black Death removed the problems of famine caused by over-population. The Dales contain many fine examples of strip lynchets, the most accessible collection being seen at the southern approaches to Linton in Wharfedale.

The medieval countryside of the Dales was a patchwork of different types of farming. Around most villages and hamlets there were the communally worked strip fields covering the pockets of ploughland. Flanking the rivers and streams were hay meadows, also divided into strips or 'doles', with strip lynchets sometimes terracing the slopes and revealing a desperate quest to obtain more arable land. Striding across the Dales and reaching up to Derwentwater and Borrowdale in the Lake District were the great monastic sheep ranges, puncuated by granges with their clusters of sheep pens and lambing paddocks. And intermeshed with these ranges were the common pastures shared by the peasant farmers. During the Middle Ages and into the eighteenth century ambitious peasant farmers attempted to enclose common land for their private uses. Sometimes the authorities and landlords turned a blind eye to these anti-social enterprises and at other times they sought to turn the tide. A legacy of these struggles are rather large irregular fields frequently seen at the junctions between the upland commons and the valley pastures. They are known as 'intakes'. Intaking was one problem faced by the farming community and squatters were another. These were impoverished families who struggled to exist by grazing a few beasts on the common, which might also provide them with peat for fuel and bracken for bedding. If they could, the squatters would seek to establish their own intakes, thus increasing their nuisance value to the more respectable members of the community. Quite often one will see straggling lines of cottages or farmsteads and these often mark the edges of old commons where families once settled to gain access to the shared grazings.

Parliamentary enclosure of the Forest of Knaresborough produced this geometrical fieldscape around Darley and Thornthwaite

Frequently these grazings were regulated or 'stinted' to balance the number of stock being raised with the capacity of resources. Many surviving commons still are controlled in this way, each farmer being allocated a number of 'gates', equivalent to a set number of sheep, lambs and cattle. Most unpopular in the old farming communities were those who attempted to bring in stock belonging to outsiders.

The history of the commons disappears into ancient times and probably began soon after the birth of farming in the Dales. In the seventeenth and eighteenth centuries, however, the privatisation of common land became increasingly fashionable. If one happened to be a prosperous landowner then the attractions of reorganising tenancies, enclosing one's share of the common and getting rid of the paupers in the farming community were obvious. If, however, one was one of these paupers or a small tenant farmer then the prospects were terrifying. This privatisation of the countryside was achieved when the leading landowners in a parish petitioned Parliament to pass an Act of Enclosure. Generally these Acts were produced on a piecemeal parish-by-parish basis, but in the 1770s the many commons and communal fields of the vast Forest of Knaresborough were subject to a single Act of Enclosure.

Parliamentary enclosure was largely achieved in the century 1750 to 1850. No other single process has so transformed the countryside or added

to the character of the Dales. In each affected parish commissioners – the leading lights in local society – and surveyors were appointed to mastermind and delimit the carve-up of commons assets. The result was a geometrical surveyor's landscape of straight-edged fields. Occasionally, where the limits of the enclosed area followed an old land boundary, the bounds would curve, but otherwise the once-open countryside became criss-crossed by a network of walls born as lines ruled on a surveyor's map. The recipients of the new holdings were required to transform these lines into walls and precise instructions were usually given about their size and construction. Smallholders who had gained pitiful little holdings which could never match the value of their former shares in the commons and who could not even afford the costs of walling would soon be found slaving as farm labourers or exchanging the moan of the wind and the shrill of the curlew for the clatter of shuttles in a mill in Bradford or Manchester.

While all this was going on the activity in the fields, lanes and little local quarries must have been enormous. Hitherto walling had been a fairly sporadic and small-scale activity and we must wonder how all the skills needed to divide hills and valleys with thousands of miles of walling were so rapidly acquired. Now these walls are darkened with age and patterned by lichen but at first they must have seemed like bright webs superimposed on old scenes, the gritstones honey-coloured and the limestones glaring white

Most of these little hedged pastures near West Burton contain a barn

and silver. Today the ageing walls are universally regarded as vital to the scene, but originally their aesthetic contribution was derided. Writing in 1878, T. D. Whitaker, a local historian, complained that the old pastures, once as large as parks, were now 'strapped over with large bandages of stone, and present nothing to the eye but right lined and angular deformity'.

The enclosure walls were built in a manner which is still practised. They have double walls of roughly squared stones which slant slightly inwards up to a height where they can be capped with a single row of 'topstones', which are often mortared in place. When met at work the drystone waller will be seen to use a very simple set of tools. A line of string marks the intended height of the wall while an 'A'-shaped wooden frame is used to set out the cross-section to be built. A hammer is used to shape the stones and the chips of stone smashed away in the shaping process are used as 'fillers' to pack the spaces between the two skins of stone. The task of drystone walling is much more difficult than it may appear to be. One of the waller's great skills is the ability to see at a glance which stone from the pile will tightly fill which niche in the wall.

The inward slope or 'batter' of the drystone wall increases its strength while the mortaring of the topstones reduces damage by those scaling the wall. Even well-built walls require repair from time to time. Some damage is caused by careless ramblers, some by frost, but gales are a major problem and in exposed places the blast may be sufficient to topple a wall. In the past most farmers had some walling skills and today numerous professional wallers find ample employment in the Dales. Unfortunately many old walls are being dismantled to create larger pastures or else allowed to tumble and decay, while much walling work is seen at the roadside in association with road-widening work or crash-damage repair.

The seasonal cycle of farming is evident in our landscapes in sights less obvious than the buttercup meadow in full bloom or the field of scurrying lambs. Stone field barns are an integral part of the scenery and in parts of Swaledale there seems to be one in every single field. These barns were essential to the old style of farming. The fields in which they stand are, or were, hay meadows and in summer when the hay was cut and dried it was swept into the convenient barn. After the hay harvest stock grazed the meadow and in winter when the grass had ceased to grow they were sheltered in the barn and fed on the store of hay. Then in spring the manure which had accumulated in the barn and its midden was taken out and spread on the meadow, thus renewing fertility for the next crop of hay. It is organic farming *par excellence* but a form of management which is in decline. Many of these little old field barns, most dating from the eighteenth and nineteenth centuries, are threatened by neglect while a further quarter are only in 'fair' condition. A recent plan by the National Park and English Heritage to designate a conservation area covering almost

800 barns in the Swaledale area is currently threatened by opposition from farming and landowning interests, who are suspicious of bureaucracy and not always sympathetic to the ideals of conservation.

Yet we must not forget that, bloody-minded as he may often be, the hill farmer is the most valuable resource in the Yorkshire Dales. Without the farmer the open fell grazings would surrender to scrubland and the commercial forestry interests would move in, carpeting the landscapes in dark plantations of conifers which thrive poorly and die but earn tax relief for rich investors as they do so. Despite subsidies at the rate of £13 per sheep, recent times have been hard for the hill farmer. In the autumn sales of 1989 mule gimmer lambs were selling at only £55 to £60, about £20 below the levels in the previous year. Southern English farmers were reluctant to buy because the summer drought had reduced their winter fodder crops while high interest rates affected all branches of the industry. These factors may not recur for some years but a succession of low prices would bankrupt countless hill farmers.

Nationwide surveys have revealed a problem of a quite different kind which faces some hill farmers – that of finding the right spouse. Social opportunities in the remote upland settings are limited and it is not always easy to meet the special kind of woman who will sacrifice the pleasures and conveniences of life in the town or village and accept the loneliness, cold, long working hours and often poverty of living far from neighbours, especially during the bleak dark days of winter.

If the nation believes that the Dales landscapes of fell pastures, walls, farmsteads and valley meadows must be preserved then it must also face up to the problems of preserving the community of farmers. By and large the members of this community treasure the settings in which they work and are prepared to accept the hardships and modest incomes in return for the freedom to remain living 'on the view'. But the survival of the hill farmer and the countryside that he maintains will have to be paid for by the taxpayer in subsidies and incentives. Piecemeal initiatives and conflicting policies cannot work. An overall strategy is needed and even then ways must be found to overcome the hill farmer's innate distrust of bureaucracy.

CHAPTER 12

Farming –
A Disappearing Age

Today the Dales is a beautiful region; thirty or more years ago it was a scenic utopia which was farmed in ways which had not changed greatly for a century and longer. Most visitors would probably assume that the great changes came earlier this century with the introduction of tractors, other farm machinery and artificial fertiliser. In fact the great changes have come more recently and they involve factors which have transformed the traditional system of mixed farming into a situation where sheep-farming is predominant and in which this last bastion of the farming way of life seems in danger of collapsing.

At the time of President Kennedy and the Beatles the typical Dales farm was still a mixed farm with chickens pecking around in the yard, hill sheep on the fell, bullocks and perhaps a few Mashams in the pastures and a dozen or so dairy cows which were led home for milking each afternoon. A few decades earlier goats were commonly kept, their rich milk being fed to sickly lambs. One by one these props to farming life have been knocked away, leaving just the fragile support of hill sheep standing in some places. The Milk Quota system favours the lowland farm with its longer growing season for grass, while as dairy farming has declined it has become less economical to collect milk from the remaining dairy farmers. The disappearance of the dairy cow has meant that calves for fattening are not being produced, so that the beef farmers must bid in auction against the wealthier lowland competitors. (Beef or 'suckler' cattle have been substituted for dairy cattle on some farms, but they are a costly purchase.) Encouraged by policies to cut their grain production, these competitors are now turning to milk and beef production – at the expense of the disadvantaged farmers in the hills.

Farming in the Dales was not always the plaything of London and EEC policies. Tradition and self-sufficiency played much greater parts. Hill farmers struggled by on tiny incomes, finding the rent for their farms (which would have averaged around £50 per annum in the 1930s) by selling a few cows, butter, eggs and lambs at the local markets while living on the products of their farms and land. Peat was dug for fuel and sometimes thin seams of low-grade coal could be mined. Bracken and rushes were scythed down and used for bedding. Chemical fertilisers could not be purchased but manure from the farmyard and barn was spread on the meadows and pastures, with lime and basic slag sometimes being bought in to neutralise the acid grazings. Almost every farm had a couple of pigs of the Large White breed, which were slaughtered each year and converted to the hams which hung as an indispensable facet of the kitchen scene.

The modern meadow is a rather unnatural place, periodically ploughed and sown with a mixture of alien rye grasses. Then it is heavily dosed with fertilisers and a uniform bottle-green harvest results, often cut early and converted into silage. The old meadows, some of which endure, were never ploughed but were packed with those grasses most strongly established in the local environment, along with wild orchids and a galaxy of wild flowers. Not being force-fed on chemicals, the older meadows matured a little later. On all but the smallest holdings the scythe surrendered to the mechanical mower early in this century. Before the Second World War these mowers were generally horse-drawn: tractors were expensive and could not always negotiate the pits, boulders and slopes of the unimproved farm tracks.

The Dales farmer could not sustain a huge and greedy heavy horse like the Suffolk or Shire which hauled ploughs across the clinging clays of the lowlands. Rather he required an economical and willing pony which would be sure-footed on the steeper slopes. This was achieved by crossing Scottish Galloway ponies with local stallions. The product was a sturdy animal usually a little over fourteen hands in height which might be black, brown, dun or grey and which gained recognition as a separate Dales pony breed in 1917. Now these tough little horses are hardly ever seen at work but a Dales × Fell pony cross is popular as a reliable mount for the young rider. The successor of the Dales pony was the tractor. Little grey Ferguson tractors appeared in the 1950s and were ideally suited to the rough conditions. Now the 'li'l grey Fergie' would be worth a place in any Dales farming museum – but quite a few are still leading active working lives.

Returning to the hayfield, haytime and lambing were – and still are – the great landmarks of the farming year. At haytime all able-bodied members of the community were conscripted to the meadows, and players devoid of any talent were suddenly welcomed into the depleted local cricket teams. Sometimes the workforce was enhanced by the employment of casual Irish workers – aptly known as 'July barbers'. Around the end of the last century the greed for labour was slightly reduced by the introduction of horse-drawn mowing machines. In the days before mechanisation each mower cherished his own scythe, sharpening it with tallow and fine sand gathered from the shores of a tarn, and each was followed by several children or adults who would rake the mown hay over their outstretched legs to make little piles of grass known as 'foot-cocks' or knee-high mounds known as 'jockeys', which consisted of two foot-cocks. This helped the grass to dry, especially if the weather was bad. The making of much taller hay-cocks or 'pikes' was common until quite recently, the sides of the pikes being combed downwards with a rake so that rain would be shed.

Before leaving the field the hay was raked into long swathes or 'windrows' either by hand-raking or by a horse-drawn hayrake or swathe-turner. Today grass is either cut early for silage or cut by a tractor-drawn mower and turned into windrows several times for drying by a rotating tractor-drawn rake.

The slopes of the valley-side meadows were often too steep to allow the use of carts or wagons and hay was 'led' or carried from the field on horse-drawn wooden frames known as sweeps and sledges. If the farmer could not afford the joiner-made article then a farm gate was lifted from its hinges and substituted. The sweep was hauled between two windrows and the hay from either side was raked in. Finally a drag rake was pulled up and down the field to collect every last wisp of hay. Now a tractor-drawn baler is hauled along the windrows and it delivers firm, brick-shaped bales of hay bound up in string. It has been a familiar feature of the Dales hay meadow since the 1960s.

Frequently the hay did not have far to travel, going not to the barn by the farmstead but to a small nearby field barn. This would be divided into a 'shippon' where a few animals were kept over winter and a 'mow' above, where their hay and fodder were stored. If the harvest was a good one then the mow would be full and the surplus hay was stored on beams above the shippon.

Sheep-farming methods have changed less than other activities on the Dales farm and there is no doubt that the Dales farmers of today could, for all the obvious differences of language, enjoy more meaningful dialogues with the monastic shepherds of the thirteenth century than they can with, say, the London yuppies of today. Even so there have been several distinct changes on the hill farm. Few holdings are large enough to employ a specialist shepherd and the hill farmer is his own shepherd, his dogs often sleeping in the kennels at the farmstead door.

The remarkable antiquity of shepherding tradition can be gauged from the fact that until around the start of the present century a system of sheep-counting numerals was in use which was based on the old Celtic language and which could have been understood by shepherds in far-off Brittany. It was also used in the Lake District and varied slightly from dale to dale, but 'yan, tan, tethera, methera, pimp' meant 'one, two, three, four, five'. It was based on counting sheep in scores or groups of twenty.

Another custom which has vanished in the course of this century is that of sheep-washing, which took place in late June before the shearing. It was done because a clean, white fleece earned a slightly higher price and fleeces were formerly soiled by the greasy salves used to counteract parasites. At many places in the Dales there were 'washfolds' or 'dubs' where the sheep were immersed in water, some being pools in fast-flowing streams, some deeps at the foot of a waterfall and some artificial ponds created by damming a beck. In Nidderdale, for instance, they existed at Stean and beside the pack-horse bridge at Birstwith, while Blea Beck on Grassington moor was a Wharfedale specimen. But the best-known example is below the falls called Janet's Foss, near Malham.

Sheep were penned in folds beside the dub and some men clad in their oldest clothes waded into the water. Men on the bank tossed sheep into the dub, back legs first, and the animals swam towards the men in midstream who scrubbed each sheep and allowed it to swim to the far shore. Even in midsummer the water in the upland becks is chilly and few workers could endure more than ninety minutes of washing work at one time.

After washing, the growth of new wool caused the old fleece to rise and shearing was normally practised within a week to a fortnight. The washing was a social occasion, but not so great a one as the shearing, with catchers and clippers hard at work in the barn and the women of the township preparing the feast. The work was divided between catchers, who dragged the sheep to the clippers, sharpeners, who put a razor edge on the black steel hand-shears, the clippers themselves and the wrappers who wrapped up the fleeces, leaving out the soiled wool from the tail and rolling the fleece, old wool outside, with a strip of wool from the neck providing a tight binding. (The soiled wool or 'doddings' from the rear of the sheep was often kept in a water butt, and the resultant liquor was regarded as a wonderful organic fertiliser for tomatoes and the like.) The clippers sat on stools and would remove the fleece intact without scratching the sheep. Those sheep with a good rise to the fleece might be clipped in under five minutes but those in a poor condition could take twenty minutes to complete. On a few farms shearing is still a social occasion but more often it is done by the farming family alone or by a shearing gang.

Modern chemical sheep dips can be dangerous pollutants but provide an effective control of lice and other skin pests and have removed the need for salving, a time-consuming activity in the eighteenth and nineteenth centuries. It was undertaken in October and involved smearing each sheep all over with a salve of tar, tallow and oil, with the mixture being rubbed into partings made at close intervals in the fleece. Salving continued to be part of the routine on some Dales farms into the 1920s and one of the

Fine countrysides, like this one near Muker in Swaledale, were the creation of the old farming methods. Note the many hay barns

benefits of washing was that it helped to remove the salve residues from the fleece.

One of the advantages of the old mixed farming way of life was that, with the exception of flour, currants and vegetables, the family was largely self-sufficient. Most members of a litter of piglets might be sold but pigs were kept to provide the bacon and ham which were the cornerstone of the diet on the Dales farm. The farmyard feathered flock kept the family in eggs, while the dairy herd ensured a supply of butter and cheese, both for home use and for sale. In pre-war times this self-sufficiency reduced the need to go to shops or market, while many farmers found it more convenient to sell to roving dealers – the heirs of the 'badgers' of earlier centuries – than to drive their stock to market. The dealers had motor transport, which the farmers usually lacked.

Cheese-making was practised wherever there were dairy cattle. Some of the local cheeses gained a high reputation and others – like the 'bang' of East Anglia, or the Whangby cheese of Wharfedale – were acknowledged to be pretty awful. In the Dales the tradition of cheese-making is a very long one and from the foundations of their monasteries onwards the monks of the north made cheese from the milk of their ewes. During the Middle Ages both cattle and sheep were milked for cheese and gradually a preference developed for the cow's milk product. One cannot know when the distinctive mild Wensleydale cheese first developed, but its name and qualities gained formal recognition at cheese fairs held at Leyburn in the middle of the nineteenth century. This was not the only cheese made in the Dales: there was a very similar-tasting Cotherstone, a blue Wensleydale deliberately infected with mould from the cheese room and the wonderful creamy and tangy Swaledale cheese. Wensleydale cheese is widely available, and locally made 'farmhouse' varieties can often be purchased at the roadside. Swaledale cheese is still the most elusive but can be found in local specialist cheese shops such as that at Aysgarth, which is from a small production at Deer Park, Harkerside. A few years ago David Reed, a chef from South Shields, decided to revive Swaledale cheese production and was fortunate to meet a farmer's wife who had preserved an old Swaledale recipe which only she remembered. Recently the cheese-making business established by David and Mandy Reed moved to an industrial estate at Richmond and to a dairy which obtains milk from two Swaledale farms. They plan to develop a Swaledale ewe's-milk cheese, which will surely resemble the cheese made in the Dales in monastic times.

Cheese-making was a farmhouse industry which involved plenty of work for the farmer and his wife but which converted milk, a very perishable product, into a form which could be stored and later taken to market or sold to a dealer. A farm with a small dairy herd of fifteen cows could produce about four cheeses a day during the main cheese-making period. Generally cows were only brought to the milking shed in winter, while in summer they were milked out in the fields where they stood. Milk was then carried back to the dairy either in heavy four- to eight-gallon 'backcans', carried on the back of the farmer's wife or dairy maid or in crates and backcans slung on the back and sides of donkeys. Milk from the afternoon milking was poured into a large copper vessel or 'cheese kettle' and kept warm overnight. Rennet was stirred in and the whey drained off, while the curds were hung in a bag to drain with some salt being added to the curds. Then a variety of presses were used to squeeze moisture from the developing cheese, which was later removed from the press, bandaged in cheese-cloth and stored on a shelf in the cheese house to ripen for a few months. Part of the character and quality came from the skills of the farming family and part was imparted by the grass and flora of the Dales pastures.

Cheese-making was not confined to the farmsteads, and various local dairies were established, buying in milk from the local farmers and producing cheeses under conditions rather more hygienic than those prevailing in some farmhouses. The first cheese factory in Wensleydale was established in 1857. One at Birstwith produced Wensleydale and Cheddar cheese of memorable quality until the 1960s and Cheddar, Cheshire and later Wensleydale cheeses were made in a converted inn in Coverdale. In the northern dales, Coverham, Dent, Hawes and Leyburn all had dairies. A small museum of cheese-making equipment has been established at the dairy at West Marton.

Butter was often a more troublesome product. The milk was churned in a barrel, either with a paddle or 'dasher' turned by a handle or by working up and down with a plunger. The time taken for the butter to form was unpredictable and after hours of hard but unproductive work some women could invoke superstition or black magic. When the butter had formed it was 'clashed' or pounded in a large bowl to remove the buttermilk, rolled into bomb-shaped divisions weighing a pound or a pound-and-a-half, rolled again into cones, rolls or oblongs and then printed using a wooden roller or stamp. Formerly each farm had its own distinctive decorative mark or stamp. As with cheese-making the flavour of the butter embodied the herbs of the pasture.

In pre-war times there was no passing tourist trade to speak of, so, like the cheese, the butter was taken to market or sold to itinerant dealers. Settle, Barnard Castle and Hawes were among the local markets for dairy goods and it is recorded that in the spring of 1878 up to 7000 pounds (3175 kg) might be traded in a good day at Hawes. Alternatively, butter and cheese could be sold to dealers or cheese factors. The factors toured the farmsteads buying cheese or bartering it for groceries and the produce was then sold on to the industrial towns, at markets outside the region or to grocer clients.

OPPOSITE ABOVE
*Wensleydale cheese
for sale at the roadside*

RIGHT
*Janet's Foss near
Malham is a former
sheep-washing site*

OPPOSITE BELOW
*Old skills are still
proudly displayed at
sheep-dog trials in the
Dales*

At the outbreak of the last war more than 400 households in the Dales engaged in the making of cheese for sale. Twenty years later the local farmhouse industry had officially become extinct. Commercial dairies had formed, amalgamated, been rationalised and taken over, while the Milk Marketing Board, founded in 1933, furthered the centralisation. The way was paved for the mass production of the bland products which sweat in their plastic wrappers on the supermarket shelves. However, the old cheese-making skills are not completely forgotten and the lively tourist traffic combined with the modern enthusiasm for 'real' foods could revive the farmhouse industry even though the keeping of dairy cattle has declined so steeply.

LOCAL CHEESE

WENSLEYDALE
MUSLIN WRAPPED

FULL £3.50p
½ £1.75

Dales farmers of the past (and present) were as tough and hardy as could be – for mere survival demanded no less. They worked for even longer than from dawn until dusk, for their toil began way before the sun had risen. Their wives were no less hardy, for while the farmer was out among his beasts, mother and daughters tended the stock around the farmhouse, milked in the fields and converted the milk into butter and cheese. It is easy to sentimentalise the past, especially if one has never experienced the rigours of farm life, the dust and sweat of the hayfield or the utter exhaustion of the lambing. True-born Dalesfolk are becoming fewer and fewer as farmsteads and cottages pass to 'off-comers' or 'off-cumdens' at prices which the older locals cannot credit. Talk to these older folk and you will learn of the ravages of stock diseases, against which the gimcrack remedies then available were largely ineffective. You will hear about life in cottages which lacked not only electricity and gas but also water, and you will discuss the many miles that people would walk to get an extra penny for their produce. But almost invariably you will also hear them say how much happier those times were, when big business and bureaucracy were kept at bay, when communities co-operated in the hayfield or at the sheepfold and when the company of honest-to-goodness neighbours was a sheer delight.

The older farmers farmed in a natural way – they neither knew nor could afford any other. Circumstances made them hard, but on the whole they treated their stock without cruelty. Cows had names, not numbers and each farmer and shepherd recognised each individual sheep in a flock. Farmers who were as tough as old boots would often pay a little extra at auction for a sheep with a prettily marked face – though they would never admit to having done so. A man was judged by the quality of his stock, his craft and his grasp of farming lore. Reputation was important and counted for much in communities which owned little else. We can only guess what the old farmers would have thought of battery farming, the breeding of grotesque calves so large that they can be delivered only by caesarian section and the feeding of cattle on offal from diseased sheep, thus creating 'mad cow' disease. Probably they would see these things as a reflection of the unwholesome nature of modern society.

PART FOUR

CHAPTER 13

Nature in the Dales

Much more of creation survives in the Dales than endures in lowland England. Fairly recent times have seen the extinction or eviction of a number of fascinating birds and animals, but for thousands of years the impact of man on the countryside had beneficial results because he added to the diversity of the environment. Prehistoric burning and grazing prevented woodland from recolonising the high fells, encouraging the spread of moorland and rough pasture, while lower down the countrysides of wood and marsh were exploited to created herb-rich meadows and pastures. In such ways new niches for a wide variety of flora and fauna were formed.

Before looking at the wildlife which remains we may examine briefly that which has been lost. The bear could have been hunted out in Roman times and does not seem to be evidenced by any surviving place-names. This is not the case with the beaver, which may have built its dams across the rivers in the region until Saxon or early medieval times. The wild boar was present in the medieval forests but its natural survival is debatable since boar were periodically introduced to hunting reserves. Legend tells that 700 years ago Thomas Ingilby was granted estates at Ripley in Nidderdale for diverting a charging boar away from his king; the family is still in residence there.

Under the natural order the lordship of the fells belonged to the red deer and its predator, the wolf. Both have been hunted to extinction in the Dales, the wolf by the end of the Middle Ages, and it is said that the last indigenous red deer and fallow deer were both killed in 1805. A small herd of red deer is maintained in Ribblesdale and its members may wander into the Forest of Bowland. At both Fountains Abbey and Bowland Priory bounties were paid for the killing of wolves during the fifteenth century and payments of 3d or 4d (1.2p or 1.7p) per night were given to servants for guarding the flocks against wolves. The name of Woodale in Coverdale may

commemorate the medieval wolf but names associated specifically with the red deer are hard to recognise – Hartwith in Nidderdale could be named after the fallow deer. In Hartwith parish there is Catstone Wood, probably named after the wildcat, a predator more recently evicted from the Dales.

Records from Victorian times tell of an animal called locally a 'fomund', and this can be identified as the pine marten, now only tenuously surviving in the most remote forests of the Scottish Highlands, Wales and Cumbria. Gamekeepers were responsible for the persecution and destruction of this and other fascinating creatures but they cannot be blamed so directly for the disappearance of the red squirrel, which was also recognised to be on the retreat by nineteenth-century naturalists. The grey squirrel, a North American species, was first introduced in Cheshire in 1876 and is commonly – and erroneously – blamed for exterminating its native, non-hibernating cousin. (The grey is not, as some maintain, a 'tree rat' but a genuine member of the squirrel family.) Red squirrel populations were prolific but also fragile and subject to unexplained declines, and the grey squirrel simply increased to fill the niches caused by the contraction of the red-squirrel population. It would be good to see a reintroduction of red squirrels to their former haunts in the Dales.

The most unforgivable loss of all concerns the persecution of the otter, which in the course of recent decades has been banished from most though not all the rivers of the Dales. Old-timers in my village tell of how they would stand quietly and watch the mother otter lead her cubs across the

Wild red deer were evicted from the fells but the field rearing of the animals for venison may soon increase

143

river bridge. In the 1950s, however, the otter hounds and their masters – outsiders all – hunted the animal to extinction on the middle Nidd before the arrival of legislation to outlaw this nauseating activity. Periodically there are rumours of the otter's return, but sightings of mink are probably responsible. Otter survive on a few stretches of the Ure, Wharfe and Bain but now the threats come from agricultural chemicals and the removal of bankside trees and vegetation, the otter's breeding chamber or 'holt' often being made as a tunnel among the roots of riverside trees.

River and Riverside

It is obvious that the rivers of the Dales differ greatly from those which meander lugubriously in the lowlands. While the churning current oxygenates the water in our rivers we do not find the great forests of weed associated with the rivers of the plains. Instead the waters are crystal clear – except when stained red by peat washed down from the moors – and the stony river beds are plainly seen. These rivers have steeper gradients, plenty of rapids and are subject to sudden and dramatic rises when cloudbursts soak the fells. Life is adapted to this turbulent regime and any weed would soon be swept away.

The water in the rivers of the Dales is still relatively pure – though not as pure as it was before the adoption of silage-making and fish-farming, the two most serious causes of pollution here. Crayfish, small lobster-like crustaceans, are regarded as indicators of good water and may still be found in several rivers.

The king of the river in the Yorkshire Dales is the brown trout. Seen from the shore it can be recognised by the profusion of dark spots on its khaki back and from the gold flash from its sides as it moves. Its size is largely controlled by the wealth or poverty of the setting. In the upper reaches of the limestone streams the fish weigh just a few ounces and elsewhere fish of more than a pound are generally considered quite good. The Wharfe is a noted angling river, but a difficult one to fish on account of the extreme clarity of the water. Many stretches of river in the Dales are restocked with rainbow trout, not a native fish and one which flashes in blue or mauve rather than the gold of its brown cousin. It is an inferior fish but one which responds more effectively to artificial rearing conditions than does the brown trout.

If the brown trout is king in the rivers of the Dales, there is also a king in exile: the salmon. Salmon would enter the rivers of the Dales via the Humber and Ouse, and the Ure was still a salmon river at the start of this century. In 1932 a salmon of 25 pounds (11 kg) was caught on the river. There are still sporadic reports of salmon entering the Ouse tributaries but any fish seeking to reach them must brave the chemical filth of the Humber and the pollution of the lower Ouse. The Ribble, however, is still a notable salmon river, the fish avoiding the poisons produced on Humberside and arriving from the west via Lytham St Anne's and Preston. They can still be seen in large numbers as they queue to leap falls and brave rapids *en route* to their spawning grounds. Sea trout also visit the Ribble.

The queen of the rivers of the Dales is the elegant grayling. It is silvery in colour with a slate-grey back and a large, sail-like dorsal fin spotted in shades of grey and deep pink. A small adipose fin between the dorsal fin and tail denotes a relationship with the trout and salmon, and the fish has a distinct scent of musk. The cool rivers of the Dales with their fast flow and good oxygenation are ideal for the grayling. These conditions are also favoured by the larger and rarer barbel, found in selected places where the rivers run clear and deep over beds of stone and sand. The barbel can grow up to 31 inches (80 cm) in length and is a long, streamlined fish of a colour shading from grey–brown on its back through bronze to cream on the belly. Small, fleshy barbels hang from the front and back of the upper lip. This powerful fish is much sought by anglers and the Dales lies at the northern extent of its range.

Less aristocratic coarse fish than the grayling or barbel are found in various reaches of the rivers. Roach are quite widespread, chub found in places like the middle Nidd, and bream occur in Semer Water. Smaller fish include the dace, gudgeon, bullhead and stone loach. While salmon, trout and grayling form the royalty of the Dales rivers, minnows are the proletariat. Visitors to the river banks in summer may be surprised to see brown clouds the size of tablecloths which cruise slowly across the shallows before suddenly dissolving into thousands of darting bodies. The clouds are shoals of spawning minnows and our rivers provide the ideal conditions of clear stony waters with marginal shallows which the humble minnow requires. The fish spawn between April and June, when even from the bank the patient observer can see the red bellies and white spots or 'tubercles' which develop on the heads of the males during the breeding season.

Fish life is made possible by the insect populations of the Dales rivers, while fish and insects support a number of attractive riverside birds. The largest of these is the grey heron, which is still sufficiently common to be seen in the course of many, if not most, long riverside walks. The birds may be seen standing stiff and still until the moment when a fish is spotted and the long, dagger-like bill stabs the water like a blade from a flick-knife. When moving to or from their nests or heronries at dawn and dusk the birds are recognised by their size – larger than any bird which may be seen bar the goose and eagle – and their large flapping wings. Herons nest in the crowns of woodland trees, building large untidy nests of sticks and rushes.

Kingfishers are more seldom seen, even in places where they are breeding. The first impact upon the visitor may be a lightning flash of

The brown trout, king of the river in the Dales, may be deposed by acid rain and the greenhouse effect for it needs cold, pure water

The grey heron

iridescent turquoise blue, and before one can register the creature's presence the bird is out of sight. This is a species of the lower reaches of fast-flowing rivers, and pairs establish territories spanning long stretches of river up and down from the nesting site, a tunnel in a high river bank well above the reach of floodwaters. Usually the bird is seen in flight, darting upstream or downstream on whirring wings, and sometimes its call, surprisingly loud and harsh, may be heard. The most fortunate and least noisy visitors may be lucky enough to see the bird fishing from a vantage point a few feet above the river, usually an overhanging branch or a piece of dead wood trapped by the boulders of the river bed. Then one can appreciate not only the brilliance of the blue wing feathers but also the orange-red breast and the speed of the bird as it plummets into the water to seize minnow or fish fry. In early autumn small groups of young birds, less worldly-wise than their parents, may be seen chattering and scolding around a riverside perch. The kingfisher is dependent on small fish, particularly the bullhead, and may starve when rivers are frozen or affected by flooding. At such times the birds may migrate downstream and seek a living in coastal margins.

Visitors who spot the kingfisher are lucky, but none should fail to see many dippers. The shape of a robin and the size of a blackbird, the dipper has its drab dark-brown plumage relieved by a bold, white bib. It will be found perched on boulders which project a few inches above the fast-flowing waters and be seen to be bobbing up and down in a jerky manner. Then the dipper will plop into the rushing waters, take a brief walk on the river bed and return with the larvae of water beetles, may flies or with water fleas or snails. Sometimes building its domed nest against rocks or roots in the river bank, the dipper also nests against walls. It is the most characteristic waterside bird of the Yorkshire Dales and only the ubiquitous mallard is seen more frequently.

Two types of wagtail, the pied and the grey, are commonly seen in the region; a third type, the yellow, with its olive back and yellow breast, is a rarer summer visitor breeding only in Britain and a few French locations. With its long twitching tail and black and white plumage the pied wagtail is unmistakable. Though originally a bird of the waterside, it has colonised weirs and millstreams and shows little fear of man. On the evidence of its name alone, the grey wagtail might be thought to be a rather drab little fellow, but in fact it is one of the most colourful of the region's birds, with a lemon yellow belly, slate back, black bib and a tail outlined in white. It is a bird of the riverside which may be seen in meadows and pastures. The yellow wagtail is interesting because it represents evolution in action and is producing variations or sub-species which may evolve into species in their own right. The 'standard' bird has a yellow breast and olive back, but several divergencies have been noted, including offspring from crosses with the blue-headed wagtail. It is a bird of damp, low-lying grasslands.

The sand martin will be less familiar to most visitors than its cousin, the house martin, whose cup-like nests are slung beneath the eaves of so many village dwellings. The sand martin, in contrast, nests in tunnels in sandy banks and the sight of birds darting from the ground may surprise the unsuspecting rambler. The sand martin is a dull brown in places where the house martin is dark blue. These birds of the swallow family catch their food on the wing and since insects hatch in large numbers from the rivers in summer one will often see tiers of sand and house martins and swallows sweeping over the riverside, with a higher tier of screeching swifts circling above. The sand martin still nests in sandy river banks in some parts of the Dales, such as Middle Wharfedale, but the drought in its wintering grounds in the southern Sahara fringe has cut its numbers by perhaps three-quarters.

In the course of a walk along the Nidd a few years ago I would expect to see at least a dozen moorhens but now I may not see one in the course of a month of walks. It had always seemed strange that a bird so vulnerable could be so successful, for the open nests, often built on small floating islands of vegetable debris trapped against a branch, expose the brown-blotched eggs to one and all. The bird has a habit of diving under a bank if trouble approaches, emerging furtively or else with much noise and panic if the trouble is genuine. The size of a small bantam and drab when seen at a distance, on closer inspection the bird is seen to have a bright-red bill with a yellow tip and two white flashes beneath its tail. As a riverside bird it is unusual in having a basically vegetarian diet, though insect food is also taken. The demise of the waterhen in many places is due to the ravages of the mink, vicious predators descended from animals which have escaped from English fur farms. How the authorities ever allowed the importation of such obviously lethal animals is almost beyond belief but now our native wildlife is paying a horrendous price for the lack of foresight and the vanity of rich women. In the space of a couple of years friends have trapped ten mink at a single spot on the Nidd, and each time a pair is removed the local waterfowl have a brief opportunity to raise young. But then new mink soon move into the hunting territory. Though seldom seen, the mink are now widespread and firmly established and one doubts that they will ever be removed. About midway in size between an otter and a stoat, the mink is usually dark brown in colour.

Despite the onslaught of the mink, mallard are still numerous and are by far the most common members of the duck family. Wild populations have frequently crossed with farmyard ducks, producing many colour variations, such as white and bi-coloured drakes and pale buff females. With its glossy bottle-green head, white neck band, brick-red throat and blue wing flash the pure-bred wild mallard drake is much more striking than any of the hybrids. Wherever tourists gather the local mallards soon learn to overcome their innate fears and beg for crumbs. Perhaps this charity over-enlarges the mallard population, for who will come to feed the ducks in the harsh days of January?

In general the fast-flowing rivers and high-level waterbodies are not to the taste of most members of the duck family. Between October and March some of the Scandinavian population of goldeneye visit the region, the drakes being recognised by the bold white spot below each eye on the dark-green head. Common scotter, red-breasted merganser and goosander also visit in small numbers. The prettiest of our native ducks and one of the most threatened is the delightful widgeon, which recently became established as a breeder on Grimwith reservoir between the dales of the Wharfe and the Nidd. In 1989 a well-orchestrated campaign involving Yorkshire Water and Leeds boating and windsurfing interests attempted to develop these disruptive activities on the lake, against the wishes of the Nature Conservancy Council, which sought to protect completely the colony of widgeon, which normally breeds much further north. The National Parks Authority accepted a compromise plan by invoking a limited ban at the most sensitive stages in the nesting season. One hopes that the ducks appreciate the difference between sanctioned and unsanctioned disturbance!

Canada geese were introduced to Britain in the seventeenth century and became established, but in the course of doing so they lost the urges to migrate and to socialise. Breeding populations of this handsome goose have been successful and can be seen at some upland waterbodies and at Gouthwaite reservoir in Nidderdale.

Of the wild flowers of the riverside, the most attractive, the marsh marigold or kingcup, seems to be less common than before. Two other plants, foreigners both, have become firmly established, the yellow monkey flower or mimulus and the rose-pink Himalayan balsam. Mimulus can be seen growing in the shade of wet rocky banks while the balsam can provide a continuous riverside fringe, each clump buzzing with bees. There is no denying the visual attractions of the balsam, originally introduced as a garden annual, but it has become so successful that native plants of the river bank have been evicted by its spread.

Finally, perhaps the most characteristic feature of the Dales river is the lines of alder which fringe each bank. The alder seems to thrive with its 'feet' half in the water, and its roots bind and help to stabilise the banks. Though unspectacular as a specimen tree and with wood once used for clog-making but now seldom considered, the alder corridors are visually and ecologically important and in winter and early spring these corridors are followed by flocks of siskins which feed on the seeds, catkins and buds. The siskin is a little olive-yellow finch with an interesting history. Until the middle of the last century the birds were rare, confined to the ancient Caledonian forest of native Scots pine in the Scottish Highlands. Perhaps the planting of larch, spruce and fir plantations provided stepping stones

The rare and lovely widgeon

A mallard drake preening

The Canada goose has developed a new lifestyle in the Dales

which helped the birds to spread. Now they can be seen in Norfolk and North Wales and have learned to visit bird tables. Some of the siskins seen in winter are visitors from the Continent.

Meadow and Field

In the classic Dales scene the river is flanked by a zone of damp hay meadows. Thus it must have been for thousands of years, as plants and animals of moist grassland habitats became slotted into the niches which man created and maintained. Sadly, however, the age-old regime of growth, drying and cutting has been widely replaced by one of cutting the grass early and green – with devastating effects upon the dependent wildlife. When some plants and creatures are exterminated, only the botanists and naturalists are aware of the loss, but in other cases an entire pillar is removed from the environmental edifice and places are never quite the same. It is as though an orchestra has lost its violas or horns. This is the case with the corncrake. The bird itself is not spectacular – it is shaped like a partridge, about 12 inches (30 cm) long and mottled in shades of buff, chestnut and grey. But the loud and grating 'crex-crex' call was a vital feature of the setting between the bird's arrival in late April and the end of July. It provided a theme tune for the Dales. During the last century the changes in life on the land – farm mechanisation, silage-making and also the erection of overhead cables which are hit by migrating birds – have evicted the corncrake from the Dales. Silage-making was the most fatal development, destroying the nests and killing the chicks before they were ready to support themselves. Now the corncrake survives in the Lake District, the Scottish Islands and Anglesey. Periodically one learns of sightings – or rather hearings – in the Dales, but the prospects for the return of the corncrake seem worse than bleak.

The grey partridge of the hedged pasture and ploughland is now in steep decline. Again the changes in farming methods are blamed while late springs, frequent in recent years, appear to deprive the hungry young chicks of food. The red-legged partridge, much more gaudy in its multicoloured markings, was introduced to Britain in 1673 and has expanded into the eastern Dales from its stronghold in the south-east. It can still be seen at close quarters when perched on wall tops and it seems to be more tolerant of the new farming practices.

Other creatures too are affected by the changes to the farming calendar. The hare is vulnerable as it has no burrow, just a rudimentary scrape or 'form'. Several litters of 'leverets' are produced annually by each doe, and although (in complete contrast to rabbits) the youngsters are born with fur and all faculties, they are vulnerable to the mowing and the removal of all grass cover.

One of the most familiar of the birds of the Dales is the lapwing or peewit, known locally as a 'pewit' or 'tewit'. All these names are apt, the first describing its flight and the others its plaintive, wailing cry. Lapwings are vulnerable in the same way that the corncrake is, but being more flexible in their choice of habitats and nesting sites – which also embrace moorland, high pasture and marshland – they are less threatened. Even so it is sad and frustrating to see the birds calling and circling over a field which one knows is destined for silage. Despite concerns about the lapwing visitors to the Dales can scarcely fail to see some. The underparts are white, the back, throat and cap a shimmering coppery green glossed with purple, but the most distinctive feature is the swept-back feathers on the head, which form a perky little crest. Ramblers on the fells may be disturbed to encounter 'lame' lapwings. To protect their young the birds mimic the effects of broken wings; follow them and they will lead you away from their nests, never letting you get quite close enough to capture them. Airborne birds will also indulge in a frenzy of screeching if one approaches too closely to their nesting sites.

Since it lives underground, the rabbit is less vulnerable to the effects of mowing, though old-time harvests were always associated with rabbit shoots as the animals dashed in panic from the last uncut portion of the field. The rabbit is not a native animal but was established in protected warrens in Norman times. Over the centuries its hardiness increased and it made a slow transition from delicacy to pest. Rabbit stew was standard fare in the Dales and even when the grazing damage caused by the animals was at its height the unpopularity of the rabbit was considerably tempered by a relish for the cheap and easily obtained meat. Myxomatosis, a virus carried by the rabbit flea, arrived in 1953 and soon the whole region was turned into a place of horror, the air polluted by the stench of decaying bodies. Formerly whole fields had seemed to be fringed by a mobile brown carpet, the rabbits being particularly numerous in riverside meadows with sandy banks ideal for burrowing. After 1953 rabbits became quite scarce but within a decade or so they could be seen again in small groups.

Today a ramble may still be marred by the sight of a stumbling affected rabbit but the animals seem to be developing a resistance. Contagion was most severe in large burrow communities and the survivors appeared to be those favouring a less social existence, living in walls or smaller communities. Once again the rabbit is common in the Dales but I know of only one place where rabbits can be seen in the numbers prevalent before myxomatosis. This is on the rugged limestone above Grass Wood near Grassington, where animals of the black or 'melanistic' form can be seen among their more numerous grey-brown relatives.

The damp meadows of the Dales were, and in many places still are, associated with a remarkable array of flora. The old meadows were not reseeded, so the varied grasses they contained were native species well adapted to the local environment. They were not heavily or unnaturally fertilised, so grass did not displace the flora, and they were not cut early, so flowers had the chance to set and spread their seed. In a typical Swaledale meadow owned by the Yorkshire Wildlife Trust the colour is provided by plants such as the bulbous buttercup, wood cranesbill and clover while marsh marigold, primrose, meadowsweet, giant bellflower, speedwell and forget-me-not flower at the hedgeside and by the stream. Betony and cowslip, cow parsley and sweet cicely are common in many unspoilt meadows. I have described how manure from the over-wintering stock was carted out of the field barns and spread across the surrounding field. This boost to fertility produces one of the finest scenes in the Dales – the buttercup meadow. In late spring and early summer acre upon acre of blooming buttercup meadows make it appear as if the countryside has been gilded. Such meadows can be seen throughout the Dales, perhaps the finest effects being found around Muker in Swaledale.

Roads usually follow the low-level ground of the riverside meadows, and the verges, which are free from grazing, present a different kind of floral pageant. The effects vary with the underlying geology, so that on the more acid sandstone the foxglove is the main eyecatcher. But it is on the limestone that the most dazzling displays are found and visitors driving along Wharfedale in the summer months cannot fail to be captivated by the floral carnival. The most frequently recurring hues are the mauve-blue of the meadow cranesbill and the soft grey-blue of the field scabious. Many other plants occur at intervals, the tall blue spires of the giant bellflower and the short rose-pink spikes of the common spotted orchid, the gigantic mauve orbs of the melancholy thistle and a host of commoner wayside plants.

Woodland

Often the steeper slopes joining the valley meadows and pastures are wooded. Such difficult ground would have been the last to experience clearance by man and his livestock, although the antiquity of most woodland in the Dales is uncertain. While superior in most respects to the countrysides of the English Midlands, one thing that those of the Dales tend to lack is the old managed woodland of giant oak, elm and lime standard and pollarded trees. On the limestones of the Dales a different form of natural 'climax' developed, a mixed woodland dominated by ash. A fragment of ancient ash woodland growing on the thin soils of a limestone pavement is preserved by the Nature Conservancy Council at Colt Park on the flanks of Ingleborough. As well as ash it includes rowan, the lovely bird cherry with its pendulous spires of white blossom, the guelder rose, sallow,

The common spotted orchid – one of a host of meadow wild flowers threatened by the new farming methods

OPPOSITE
A green lane near Arncliffe with verge, spring and walls providing different wildlife habitats

elder, hawthorn and soft-leaved wild rose. Other botanically notable woods include Grass Wood and Strid Wood, both in Wharfedale. Grass Wood was the medieval hunting reserve of the lords of Grassington, but in both cases the natural vegetation has been considerably altered. Many other old woods in the Dales have been quite transformed by replanting during the last century or so, with the native trees being felled and the interiors replanted with alien evergreens or with the larch and beech combination so popular in the days of the great estate, giving commercial timber and pheasant cover. Frequently an old wood name and a fringe of hazel and old pollards remain to reveal the vintage of the wood. Scrubby hawthorn woodland can be seen on a few barren slopes and birch woodland may also be found – as on the slopes below Brimham Rocks – to recreate the appearance of the countryside as it was during the early stages of recolonisation by woodland.

The old woods of the Dales contain a splendid array of wild flowers, bluebells, ramsons and wood anemone in abundance, but also some notable rarities. One of these is the globe flower with its large yellow cups, which is popular as a garden cultivar. It can be found both in damp pastures and in woodlands, like Colt Park or the little Yorkshire Wildlife Trust Globe Flower Wood reserve about a mile to the west of Malham Tarn (where visitors need not and should not cross the boundary wall). Another plant which is popular in the garden but rare in the wild is the lily-of-the-valley, found in Colt Park and in the Yorkshire Wildlife Trust Grass Wood reserve. Baneberry, wood cranesbill, water avens, variegated pansy, giant bellflower, herb Paris, melancholy thistle, primrose and blue moor grass are other plants of the limestone ash-wood habitat. The last surviving British colony of the lady's slipper orchid survives in a secret and closely guarded location in the Dales; in the eighteenth century the plant was still sufficiently common for bunches of the flowers to be sold at the Settle market.

The birdlife of the typical Dales wood may include a selection of tits, the blue, great and coal varieties being common, the marsh tit rarer. Great spotted and green woodpeckers scour the trunks for insects and grubs, along with the smaller nuthatch and tree creeper, and woodcock are not uncommon in the Dales. During the summer a number of migrant warblers may be found, along with pied and spotted flycatchers. Woods also provide shelter for the fox and the badger, the woodland cover being more extensive on the moister soils of Nidderdale. Hungry foxes have been known to take sickly lambs, so foxes are not liked by many Dales farmers. Yet fox hunts do not seem to be particularly popular either as the packs are known to cause great distress among the flocks; the activity – one cannot call it a sport – is most common on estates where tenant farmers have little say in the matter. Badgers are much less rare than one might imagine – although it is quite possible to live a lifetime in a badger locality yet never see one of these strongly nocturnal animals. Though seldom glimpsed, they

are held in great affection by most Dalesfolk. One learns in conversation that if caught by locals those louts who come from the industrial towns to dig out badgers for badger-baiting can expect an even harsher fate than others caught rustling sheep.

Although the truly wild red deer of the open fell are long extinct, the region surely contains more deer than it did in the Middle Ages. Fallow deer are creatures of woodland and the adjacent pastures and were introduced by the Normans to stock their hunting reserves. Over the centuries fallow deer have become established in the wild, where they are shy, elusive and not uncommon. The typical adult is a golden brown with white spots but the colour range goes from near black to white. In Nidderdale, for example, rather dark animals may be the offspring of escapees from Ripley deer park while the large herd at Studley Royal, near Fountains Abbey, is spotted and of a whitish-gold hue. Smaller than the fallow deer and lacking such flamboyant headgear is the furtive and solitary roe deer, the only native deer found wild in the Yorkshire Dales. Though present in some woods, roe deer are likely to be seen by only the most stealthy and patient of observers.

There is little doubt that the most remarkable of all the animals in the Dales is the sika deer. It is related to the red deer, with which it will hybridise, but is closer to the fallow deer in stature – about the size of a small donkey. The form of the antlers is more akin to the red deer rather than having the broad, 'palmated' shape of the fallow antlers, and the colour is reddish to dark brown with prominent white patches on the rump. When disturbed the fallow is likely to 'pronk' or perform a stiff-legged jump to warn its fellows, before running away, while the sika may either dash noisily away or stand and frown at the intruder. The first sika deer in Britain were brought from Asia to London Zoo in 1860. About half a century later Lord Ribblesdale of Gisburn Park introduced the sika deer to the Dales, and subsequently the deer have become established in the woods and fields of the Forest of Bowland. Several farmers have treated the animals with remarkable tolerance and the visitor may be surprised to see a sizeable herd of sika deer standing in pastures where one would expect to see nothing more unusual than black and white cows.

Moor and Mountain

Ascending steep, wooded slopes one may emerge into an area of seemingly barren limestone pavement. This is an illusion, for the pavement is a fascinating assemblage of little habitats. While the 'paving stones' or 'clints' may be bare and exposed to the full glare of the sun they are outlined by troughs or solution hollows known as 'grykes', where there is shade and moisture and where woodland and streamside plants may flourish free from the stresses of grazing. When exploring such grykes one may find herb Robert, shining cranesbill, wood anemone, wood sorrel, lily-of-the-valley, and ferns such as spleenwort, rigid buckler, brittle bladder and hart's tongue. Meanwhile the common lizard may be seen basking on the glaring white surface of a clint or darting into the safety of a gryke.

It would be difficult to choose a flower suitable as an emblem of the Yorkshire Dales, for there are several strong candidates, all of which may be found growing in or beside a limestone pavement. The lady's slipper orchid is now too rare to qualify as a candidate but the bird's-eye primrose can be found in limestone country from relatively low streamside situations to heights of up to 1700 feet (518 m). It is a dainty primrose with lilac-pink flowers in an umbel of ten or more blooms held on a slender stem. Then there is the globe flower, already described, and the bloody cranesbill with its profuse display of crimson flowers. A few years ago I bought some seed and grew it as a curiosity but now it is a valuable member of the border community, no less showy than the celebrated garden hybrids. Another candidate is the burnet rose with its creamy-white blooms held on erect, densely thorned stems. Britain contains many wild-rose species and most are hard to identify, but the burnet is quite distinctive, and even when not in bloom the forest of needle-like thorns and the black hips leave no basis for confusion. It may be found growing at altitude but will also hold its own in the competitive rough and tumble of the lowland hedgerows – see for example the riverside hedgerow between the Ribble bridge and village at Sawley. The last of the contenders must be the cheerful little mountain pansy. This plant is found in limestone uplands where free lime has been leached out of the surface soil. Ramblers are familiar with the eternally twitching yellow flowers, but the mountain pansy shows a number of colour variations, violet and yellow or brownish examples being found, while the rare Teesdale violet is a delicate violet-blue shade.

Sharing the high slopes and plateaux with the mountain pansy is the common rock rose, another yellow flower which has colour variations, in this case white and copper forms. The high pastures also provide a refuge for several wild orchids, some of which have been driven from the lower grasslands by the increasing use of fertilisers. One cannot be sure which still survive but the following orchids were quite recently enduring at altitude: greater and lesser butterfly, small white, fragrant, broad- and narrow-leaved helleborine, common and lesser twayblade, frog, heath spotted, bog, northern marsh, common spotted, early purple and fly.

In the gritstone area and also on the limestone which is blanketed in lime-free glacial drift the high plateaux are areas of bog and moorland which create scenes strikingly different from the close-cropped grazings of the limestone. Here there are 'mosses' or basins in which water collects and beds of peat form from the dead and sodden vegetation. The characteristic

A sika stag frowning at an intruder

The barren appearance of this limestone pavement is deceptive for the grikes contain a wealth of plant life and probably lizards too

The bloody cranesbill

The burnet rose

plants of such spongy environments are cotton grass and sphagnum, the unimpeded wind ever tugging at the white plumes of the cotton grass. On the better-drained peat beds one finds heather moorlands, with two forms of heather, the cross-leaved heath and the bell, also bilberry and perhaps crowberry, cowberry or craneberry as well as rushes, sedges and bracken.

Such moors are the haunts of the adder, the grass snake preferring lower, lusher places. When walking the moors in summer it is as well to be aware of the presence of adders, though the snake is more threatening to dogs than to humans. Usually it slinks away unseen but may be found basking on boulders by the lighter-footed ramblers. All three types of newt are present in the Dales, the protected great crested being localised, but the little palmate, recognised by the thread-like tip to the male's tail and webbed feet, is quite common in damp upland areas.

The heather moors of the Pennines are maintained by the grouse-shooting interest and the management involves controlled burning or 'swaling' to encourage the production of the lush, young heather shoots which the birds relish. It is this burning which produces the patchwork appearance of black, newly burned areas, green regrowth and mauve mature zones. The native red grouse is a British race of the Continental willow grouse. The eggs are laid in April in a sheltered hollow at the moorland edge and by August young birds will often be seen perching tamely on the top of walls awaiting the ensuing slaughter. The black grouse is a much more impressive bird which nests in heather and in plantations. The female is rather drab, the male much larger, up to 24 inches (60 cm) in length, and he has glossy, black plumage with a white tail, covered when it is not displaying its black, lyre-shaped tail feathers. These displays involve fighting and calling among the cock birds and begin in January or February at established 'lekking' grounds. The mating displays are sometimes revived in the autumn.

Skylark and meadow pipit nest among the tussocks at the moorland edge and several wading birds move up to the moors to breed. They include the golden plover, with its splendid black and gold summer plumage, which winters on wetlands and lowland pastures, where it is joined by migrant communities from Iceland and the Continent. Though it is sometimes regarded as a rare bird, some 7500 pairs breed in Yorkshire alone. Other waders which may be seen on the moorland and high pastures include the dunlin, snipe, redshank and curlew. The plaintive wail of the curlew is still a vital facet of the countryside experience, although changes in the management of the lower grasslands are restricting the breeding territories to the rough upland pastures. Another distinctive bird of the Pennines is the wheatear, a bird about the size of a robin with, in the male, a grey back, pinkish buff underparts and a black eye-band outlined above in white. The disappearance of closely grazed sheep pastures has caused the wheatear, which feeds on insects in short pasture, to decline in the south of England but it remains strong in the north. It nests in hollows under stones, in walls and in rabbit warrens and breeding pairs of wheatears can generally be seen among upland rabbit colonies.

While the Dales lack some of the rarer butterfly and moth species found in the warmer south, most of the common colourful butterflies are present. Most noteworthy are the moth-like skipper butterflies which may be seen in the wild-flower pastures along with others such as the ringlet, the green hairstreak and small heath butterflies of the moor and high pasture and the spectacular emperor moth, which flies at speed above the moorland clumps and tussocks.

On the highest ground the climate becomes almost sub-Arctic and it is here that the descendants of plants which colonised a warming Britain as the ice sheets melted may still be found. The alpine bistort of the limestone mountain grazings is an alpine arctic plant, as is the spring gentian, noted for the intensity of the blue colouring of its small, trumpet-like flower. Two other relics of the late glacial flora, the sea plantain and the thrift or sea pink are mainly familiar as seashore plants but also occur in the higher Pennines. The juniper, sometimes found growing in grykes, is a relic from the coniferous forest which covered much of the region after the way had been paved by the hardy plants of the tundra, while as the climate continued to improve, mixed woodland was established in the Pennines at heights up to 2000 feet (610 m). Plants from the floor of this long-vanished woodland, like the wood anemone, wood sorrel and bluebell, still linger in sheltered upland locations.

Birds of Prey

If you glance up at the skies above the highest ground, any very large soaring bird could be a golden eagle or a raven. In the past both have been ruthlessly persecuted by gamekeepers but the golden eagle has established a toehold in the Lake District, from where young birds on exploratory flights sometimes overfly the Dales. It was exterminated in the Lake District by gamekeepers a century ago but a breeding pair returned in 1968, since which time about fifteen eaglets have been successfully reared. Eagle-watchers based at Gouthwaite reservoir in Nidderdale have been rewarded by the sight of young birds making exploratory flights in the autumn. One such bird which spent a fortnight in the Dales was found dead beneath high-voltage electricity cables in 1988. The raven nests in the Lake District and northern Pennines and feeds on carrion from dead sheep and lambs; it would probably be well established in the Dales were it not for gamekeepers associated with the grouse-shooting interests. Another rare bird which may be seen in the Dales is the osprey. It breeds in the Scottish Highlands but

Dallowgill, a typical gritstone moor with heather and bracken and rowan trees in the sheltered valley

may be spotted as a bird of passage, pausing to seize fish from the reservoirs of the Dales *en route* to or from the Highlands, an area recolonised by the osprey in the 1950s. About twenty to thirty pairs of osprey breed in the Highlands, some crossing the Dales in late spring and again in the autumn, while non-breeding migrants from Scandinavia add to the numbers.

Midway in size between the eagle and the common birds of prey is the buzzard. All birds of prey suffered enormously from the use of agricultural pesticides, notably DDT. Existing at the top of the food chain, the birds died or produced infertile eggs as pesticide residues from their prey became concentrated in their bodies. The outlawing of some substances has allowed the population of several birds of prey to recover significantly, but the

residues are still detected and can lead to the laying of infertile eggs. The buzzard has suffered badly from this and other serious setbacks. In 1954 Britain contained some 12,000 breeding pairs, but as myxomatosis struck the rabbit population the buzzard lost its main source of food. Birds retreated into the upland areas and fed on sheep carrion and then fell victim to the toxic chlorinated hydrocarbons used in sheep dips. More recently the partial recovery of the rabbit population has helped to sustain a revival of the buzzard. Look out for a brown bird resembling a small and rather untidy eagle with broad wings which quarters the ground in search of prey.

During the nineteenth century the buzzard was severely persecuted by gamekeepers but the hen harrier, which has a great partiality for the chicks of red grouse, was slain to such an extent that it was eliminated from mainland Britain and confined to Orkney and the more distant Scottish Islands. Gradually, however, the hen harrier has re-advanced from its island refuges. The first time I saw one of these birds, on the edge of Masham Moor in upper Nidderdale, I was mystified as to the identity of the hawk-like creature which was larger than a kestrel but smaller than a buzzard and which was hunting low and perching on fence posts. There are great differences between the sexes, the male being distinctive in his pale-grey plumage while the larger female is brown above and buff-streaked with russet beneath. The nest is built on the moorland ground of rushes and heather.

The most dramatic of the birds of prey in the Dales is the peregrine falcon. This species suffered terribly from the pesticide catastrophe of the 1950s and 1960s, but when some of the worst chemicals were banned, Britain became a base from which the fragile population could recover. Breeding pairs are established at secret sites and it is in Wharfedale that the visitor is most likely to glimpse the peregrine. The birds are still under threat from egg collectors and falconers, while racing pigeon fanciers are believed to be flying birds baited with poison. This is because pigeons and doves feature prominently in the prey of the peregrine, along with grouse, rooks, jackdaws and even other birds of prey. They are caught in the most dramatic manner, the birds flying high in search of their quarry and then folding their wings against their bodies and plummeting at breathtaking speed to seize the prey in full flight. The falcon nests on steep, craggy scars, though it is also known to nest on the ground.

The two most common hawk-like birds in the region are the kestrel and the sparrowhawk, the latter having suffered more severely from the pesticide crisis (both the cuckoo and the increasingly common collared dove can be mistaken for hawks when in flight). Most people seem unable to distinguish between these two predators although the differences are quite marked. Any russet and slate-coloured bird seen hovering is sure to be a kestrel, for this small falcon hunts by hovering above open ground in

PREVIOUS PAGE
ABOVE
The spectacular emperor moth

BELOW
The little owl, introduced in Victorian times, persecuted by gamekeepers but still often seen perched on posts in the Dales

search of rodents and small birds. Its eyesight is obviously quite remarkable. The sparrowhawk, in contrast, is a hunter of the woods and hedgerows and will fly low and at speed to seize any small birds which are flushed from cover. The breast is barred whitish and slate and the back is grey in the male and brownish in the female. Glimpsed briefly – as is usually the case – the sparrowhawk is darker than the kestrel, often seen as a slaty-brown flash. Seen more closely it is the embodiment of aggression, the ultimate wild thing, and the gradual recovery of the sparrowhawk population is greatly welcomed. About 2 inches (5 cm) shorter than the sparrowhawk is the lovely little merlin, which hunts mainly by launching fast, low-level attacks on flocks of small birds, although it has been known to take birds larger than itself, like the red grouse and lapwing. There are only about 600 pairs of this falcon breeding in the uplands of Britain, a portion of this population surviving in the Pennines.

All the resident British owls can be seen in the Dales, the tawny owl being much the most common. It prefers wooded countryside and places with plenty of field and hedgerow trees and is abundant in Nidderdale. This is the owl which produces the familiar 'Tu-whit, tu-whoo' call (as well as a sharper 'kee-wick') and in autumn, when young tawny owls are being driven out to establish their own hunting territories, something akin to quadrophonic hooting can be heard in Nidderdale. The little owl is quite common, although its diminutive size, comparable to that of a kitten, makes it less conspicuous. It hunts both in daylight and in the evening, favouring hedged fields and waste ground, and is most easily seen when perched on fence posts and telegraph poles. The little owl was introduced in Victorian times, then persecuted by gamekeepers in the belief that it took young pheasants, but now about 10,000 breeding pairs are established in Britain with a sizeable population in the Dales. It feeds mainly on worms and insects, particularly beetles.

The ghostly barn owl has sadly decreased in the Dales, the reason for its decline lying in a complex combination of factors: it suffered very severely from the pesticide crisis, like other owls it is vulnerable to being struck by cars when hunting, and the conversion into houses of so many of the region's barns where formerly the birds nested must also have played a part in the reduction of its population. However, Britain lies at the northern extreme of the range of this widely distributed bird and there is recent evidence that the winter weather patterns of the last few decades may also be involved. Essentially a bird of warmer climes, the barn owl is unable to accumulate the fat reserves which would sustain it when winter snowfalls suspend its hunting operations. In recent years there have been reports of barn owls returning to their former haunts in the Dales; some of the birds concerned have been released as part of reintroduction projects, but others seem to be natural colonists. While the tawny tends to hunt by pouncing from the tree perch, the barn owl flies low along hedgerows, and this mode of hunting may help identification. Tawny owls vary in colour and some very light individuals may be mistaken for barn owls, but the blood-chilling shriek of the barn owl cannot be mistaken.

Mainly a resident of the northern and eastern parts of England, the long-eared owl is one of the few birds which flourish in coniferous plantations. It is very seldom seen, being strictly nocturnal in its habits and living high up in old crow and magpie nests. When disturbed it may adopt a most peculiarly elongated upright stance, its dark-brown plummage blending with the branches. Occasionally the chattering of small birds mobbing this predator may betray its presence.

The short-eared owl is a creature of very different habits and along with the kingfisher and peregrine it ranks as one of the jewels in the ornithological crown of our region. It is a bird of open moorland country which hunts during the day and is therefore quite conspicuous as it quarters its territory for food in the same manner as the hen harrier. Its diet is very varied, ranging from grouse chicks to insects, worms, young rabbits and small birds. The nest is made in a shallow scrape among the heather. At present the short-eared owl population seems secure, although it fluctuates greatly according to the successes and failures of its prey. Other British owls can be bred in captivity to produce offspring for reintroduction to the wild but the spectacular soaring courtship flight of the short-eared owl cannot be reproduced in the confines of an aviary.

The Dales is an area rich in wildlife when compared to almost all other English regions. Nevertheless too much has been lost and much more is threatened by changing practices on the farm and by development pressures. The corncrake and the lady's slipper orchid have almost gone the way of the beaver and pine marten and it would be unforgivable if treasures like the peregrine, the bird's-eye primrose or the otter were lost completely from the Dales. Pious words are one thing and the need for purposeful planning another.

PART FIVE

CHAPTER 14

Swaledale

In broad scenic terms at least, Swaledale must be my favourite dale. It embodies all the finest facets of the landscape of the Dales and combines them in vistas which are quite magical. It encapsulates all that is best in the much broader bounds of the region. The views seen as one descends into Swaledale via the Oxnop pass from Wensleydale or via West Stones Dale from the north combine everything that the exile would remember and most cherish. It is the most northern of the main dales of Yorkshire and is only atypical in so far as it tends to draw its weekend visitors from the industrial worlds of Tyneside and Teesside rather than from the Leeds–Bradford and Manchester conurbations.

From the Richmond gateway, the B6270 provides the main thoroughfare along Swaledale and we can follow it westwards past Hag Wood, the word 'Hag' denoting medieval woodland; a branch from the road leads south-wards via Downholme to Leyburn and Wharfedale. While exploring the countryside it is worth dipping into old guide books, both to discover facts about the past and to relish the overblown language. Writing of this locality in 1906, Gordon Home explained:

> The dale becomes huger and steeper as the clouds thicken, and what have been merely woods and plantations in this heavy gloom become mysterious forests. The river, too, seems to change its character, and become a pale serpent, uncoiling itself from some mountain fastness where no living creatures, besides great auks and carrion birds, dwell.

Great auks in Swaledale? Steady on, Gordon. To the north of the Swale and accessible via the bridge at Grinton is Marrick, where the remains of the nave of the twelfth-century priory of Benedictine nuns founded by Roger de Aske still stand just to the south of the village. When it was dissolved in 1539 a prioress and twelve nuns were in residence; now it is a property of the Ripon diocese and serves as a residential Youth Centre. A small priory of Cistercian nuns, now marked only by a ruined tower, lies across the river at Ellerton. Formerly, stepping stones in the Swale allowed members of the two communities to meet.

The villages of Grinton and Reeth face each other on the south and north banks of the Swale. The church at Grinton is a large one which grew during the Middle Ages from a Norman foundation. More than 20 miles (32 km) long and embracing some 50,000 acres (20,235 ha), the old parish of Grinton was one of the largest in England and this reveals how sparsely Swaledale was populated. Until a church was built further up the dale at Muker, Grinton church served almost the whole of Swaledale and was reached by a long corpse road extending to the head of the dale; pall-bearers carrying a wicker casket might spend several days on their grim mission before the tower of Grinton came into view.

Visitors in search of souvenirs could well pause at Grinton to discover refreshingly genuine local crafts. Stef and Steve Ottervanger became established in Grinton in 1985 and developed their model craft industry with help from COSIRA (Council for Small Industries in Rural Areas). They set up a workshop in Reeth and a shop by the church in Grinton producing remarkably accurate models of local working dogs and sheep. Stef makes the lifelike originals and castings are made from self-hardening plaster and then hand-painted. Now the models are exported to Wales, Holland and the USA and span more than twenty breeds of sheep and every type of dog. At Grinton the best-selling models are still the local Border collies and the Swaledale sheep, all portrayed in a way which will satisfy the most critical Dales farmer.

Across the river and between Grinton and Reeth the old Dales road, once a pack-horse track, leads back towards Richmond, via Marske, a picturesque village with a wooded backdrop. This was the ancestral home of the Hutton family which produced an Archbishop of York and Canterbury in the eighteenth century. Reeth is an old market centre whose commercial position was formalised in 1695 when Lord Wharton obtained a charter granting a weekly market and four annual fairs. The market lapsed at the end of the last century when the local lead industry decayed but in recent times Reeth has found its salvation in the tourist trade. This may be a rather mixed blessing; not so long ago the large and unusual sloping village green was a splendid sight, but now on summer weekends it tends to be masked by cars. A folk museum of life in the dale in former times is housed in the old Methodist Sunday School building and the fell race has been revived. To enjoy a fine distant view of the stone-built village recross the river and head south-eastwards on the climbing track to Leyburn which divides the moors of Ellerton and Preston.

Above Reeth the character of Swaledale becomes established, with the

OPPOSITE ABOVE
A lonely farmstead on the Oxnop Pass above Muker

OPPOSITE BELOW
In early summer buttercups turn Swaledale pastures bright yellow; this is a scene near Thwaite

gentle wooded country yielding to bare fells, grey scars and walled pastures, while the river which sparkles innocently in summer can become a furious torrent in winter. From Reeth a road heads to the north-west along the tributary valley of Arkengarthdale. This is an attractive place, but also now rather bleak and empty. The name of the dale probably means 'a small field or paddock belonging to Arkill', the unknown field-owner presumably being of Viking descent. However, though lonely, what other valley can boast hamlets named Booze and Whaw? Recent research has shown that the Methodists of Booze were not furtive drinkers: the name of their hamlet is a contraction of 'bull house'. A small church owned by the convent of Egglestone in Teesdale is said to have stood at Arkle Town, but now the dale is served by a church at Langthwaite built in 1818. Lead may have been mined in Arkengarthdale by the Romans but the heyday of lead-mining came in the post-medieval centuries, lasting until a collapse of lead prices in 1829. The larger of the mines struggled on until the cheapness of imported metal caused their demise in the 1870s and 1880s. Now the old workings, ruined buildings and Arkengarthdale's C.B. Hotel – named after the old Charles Bathurst or C.B. Mines – remain as monuments to times when the dale bustled with activity.

The Arkengarthdale road loops around to rejoin Swaledale near Thwaite, with a branch heading away to the north-west. At this road junction is Tan Hill, famed as the highest inn in England and standing at a

Reeth seen from the Leyburn track

height of 1732 feet (528 m). Numerous visitors drive considerable distances in order to be able to boast of drinking in this place and while things which purport to be the highest, oldest, smelliest or whatever tend to be suspect, Tan Hill has some genuine interest. From medieval times until the 1930s it was a local centre of coal-mining, the coal exported to lead smelters, bought by pedlars and also sold to local farmers. During the thirteenth century coals from this Crow Coal seam were worked for the lords of Richmond Castle while in the seventeenth century they were carried by pack-horse to fuel the fires at Appleby Castle, about 20 miles (32 km) away. In Victorian times a character called Elkanah used a team of donkeys to carry the coals to far-flung farmsteads, blowing a horn to announce the imminent arrival of the bizarre cavalcade. This bleak and remote place was also a venue for local sports, some of them rough and bloody, while the Tan Hill sheep show and sale has survived into modern times.

Just to the west of Reeth is Healaugh, probably the centre of an enormous Norman manor which extended from the wilderness of Arkengarthdale westwards to the headwaters of the Swale. In this middle section of the dale the influence of the lead-mining industry was enormous, hamlets like Kearton and Blades developing in association with nearby mines; Feetham supported an inn where pall-bearers bound for Grinton could rest, while Low Row hamlet was home to the novelist Thomas Armstrong, who described local customs in his book *Adam Brunskill*. Close to Healaugh the Swale is joined by the Barney Beck, which becomes the Mill Gill Beck in its higher reaches. By the beck are the remains of the Long Gang and Old Gang lead-mines and the Surrender smelter and furnace flues which travel up the fellside for 2300 feet (700 m). In March 1990 the National Park, English Heritage and the Historic Buildings and Monuments Commission agreed to begin rescue work to restore the old hushes and other relics of the industry which roofed Windsor Castle and cathedrals in Britain and on the Continent. The effects of the decline of the lead industry are most evident at Gunnerside, a village which was greatly expanded as mining developed, but which emptied as the mines collapsed. In more prosperous times its Methodist church was built with a capacity for 500 worshippers.

As one moves deeper into the Dales the scenery becomes ever more delightful. Between Gunnerside and Muker the track across Oxnop Common to Askrigg, an old drove road, offers wonderful views back into Swaledale, looking up the river to the north-west, where a field barn stands sentinel over every single field, northwards towards Ivelet and Gunnerside, where the walls outline the intricate field mosaic, and southwards to Melbecks Moor where the old workings stand desolate and bleak.

On the outskirts of Muker the valley road deserts the Swale, and the three most enticing villages in the dale, Muker, Thwaite and Keld, stand slightly apart from the river. Muker is still a riverside village, for it lies beside Muker Beck. Around 1580 Muker became the religious focus for the upper part of the dale with the building of a small thatched chapel of ease above the banks of the beck. This allowed Muker to deputise for Grinton and removed many of the Dalesfolk's hardships associated with the old corpse road.

Between Muker and Thwaite a road leads steeply up to the watershed on Abbotside Common before descending to join Wensleydale near Hawes. This is the Buttertubs Pass road, named after the giant potholes which lie right at the roadside. These potholes have formed where streams moving across the alternating strata of the Yoredales rocks have encountered a band of limestone and dissolved passages in the yielding rock. The five Buttertubs lie in a row, the two deepest potholes plummeting to depths of around 65 feet (20 m). The horizontal level of the strata and the presence of many vertical cracks and joints have allowed the rims of the gaping pots to be eroded in a strange ribbed and fluted manner so that the chasms seem to be edged in square pillars of unequal height. Having dripped or cascaded to the stone-strewn floors of the pots, water enters narrow fissures and emerges but a short distance downstream.

Thwaite is a picturesque stone village which stands beside a bridge spanning a turbulent tributary of the Swale. Here is the cottage birthplace of the famous Kearton brothers, Richard and Cherry, probably the greatest pioneers of nature photography. Richard was born in 1862 and Cherry in 1871. Although most of their films and books were concerned with the wildlife of foreign places they acknowledged that it was in this magical corner of Swaledale that they developed their love of nature. As adults they would periodically return to stay with their friends, the Harker family, in a cottage beside Muker church. In Swaledale they explored the technique of photographing birds and animals from hides, some of them of a quite bizarre and ambitious form, and it was Cherry's films and broadcasts which provided many people with an introduction to the incomparable richness of the natural world. He was killed outside Broadcasting House during an air raid in 1940.

At Keld the valley road returns to the banks of the Swale. This is the first and last village in the dale, but its isolation is breached by that most famous long-distance footpath, the Pennine Way, which arrives via Hawes and Thwaite, crosses the Swale beside Keld and then heads northwards to Tan Hill and a crossing on the Greta near Bowes. Near Keld the Pennine Way is crossed by the east-to-west track of the 'Coast-to-Coast' walk from St Bees to Ravenscar. So now the sounds of tramping boots are heard with a frequency which would never have been thought possible after the collapse of the local industry a century or so ago. In the Keld locality the Swale bucks and prances like a lively colt, and falls, rapids and ravines abound; there is the 30-foot (9-m) drop at Kisdon Force and, west of the village, there are eight cascades of which Wainwath Force is the most impressive. Above Keld the traveller may take the Tan Hill road or continue on the B6270 bound for Kirkby Stephen and Cumbria.

So far as we know it, the history of Swaledale is simple. It is the story of a spectacular but lonely backwater so thinly peopled that for centuries it could scarcely support a church. Then in post-medieval times the dramatic expansion of the ancient lead industry caused the old hamlets to swell, so that wherever one walked one would meet the miners, knitting and

Few if any villages have settings as lovely as those of Thwaite and Muker

coughing on their ways to and from the shafts and smelters. Over a century ago the industry died, and places were left desolate and derelict. But it was about this time that the first stirrings of the tourist industry were felt and inns which had served miners, drovers, pedlars and pall-bearers discovered a new clientele. While one may grumble about the military ranges and conifer plantations at the eastern end of the dale, most of Swaledale remains miraculously unspoiled and one can only hope – perhaps naively – that it may remain so. There is just so much which could be lost in this place of fragile beauty.

A typical Swaledale view with farmstead, field barns and abandoned mine-workings above

CHAPTER 15

Wensleydale

While the scenery of Swaledale is exceptional, the individual places of specific interest are relatively few. In Wensleydale the reverse situation applies. By the high standards of the Dales the scenery is generally, though not always, merely fair, but places of interest are many. Of course it must be said that not everybody would agree with this assessment of Wensleydale's scenery. Both John Wesley and Charles Kingsley considered it to be the most beautiful of the Dales and Kingsley believed this 'beautiful oasis in the mountains' to be 'the richest spot in all England'. This is undoubtedly the dale of which strangers are most aware. Everybody has heard of Wensleydale cheese, and most of the popular James Herriot television programmes are filmed in Wensleydale (although the bridge and water-splash so often seen are in Arkengarthdale). To set the record straight, James Herriot is actually Alf White and the base for his practice was not in Wensleydale at Askrigg but at Thirsk, far away to the east in the Vale of York. Nevertheless Dalesfolk born and bred will readily acknowledge that James Herriot has captured the personality and outlook of the old Dales farmers in a most perceptive and sympathetic manner – and the over-exploitation of the Herriot factor is no fault of the author's.

In contrast to much of Swaledale, Wensleydale is good farming country, the floor of the valley is rich, broad and verdant and the slopes are seldom walled by scars, so that the aura of Wensleydale is more airy and expansive. Below Wensley and Leyburn this scenic aura becomes quite un-Daleslike, a blend of parkland and mixed farming country which gently blends into the flat and rather tedious agri-business world of the Vale of York.

Visitors arriving from the south can say their thankless goodbyes to the A1 at Leeming Bar or Scotch Corner, but it is far better to make a memorable arrival to the dale via Ripon and Masham. Before reaching Masham on the A6108 one passes through West Tanfield (its former neighbour, East Tanfield, being a lost village in an area devastated by the Tudor clearances for sheep). West Tanfield is a much photographed place, the red roofs and buff walls of the cottages and the tower of the church seen reflected in the waters of the Ure. Beside the church stands the fifteenth-century gatehouse built by the Marmion family and – against all the precepts of military engineering – it is overlooked by the church tower. The Marmion family provided the Royal Champions of England from Norman times until the reign of Edward I and the tomb effigies of several medieval Marmions can be seen in the church.

At Masham one can begin a tour of discovery which underlines the claim that Wensleydale is richly studded with places of genuine interest. Apart from the historic features previously noted in this little-spoilt market town (see Chapters 6 and 9), Masham is just the place to buy those holiday presents. It has what one might least expect to find – a glassblower's workshop, producing vases and goblets streaked in a multitude of pastel shades. The workshop has a shop adjoining and the stages of glassblowing are on public display. It lies in an alley beside the large market square, with a potter's shop and workshop near by.

Beyond Masham, the A6108 heads north-westwards to the south of the River Ure through a pleasant parkland countryside and close to the remains of Jervaulx Abbey. The relics are far less extensive than those of the other great Cistercian foundations like Fountains and Rievaulx but the wild flowers and herbs growing among the ruins create a pleasant, summery aura. East Witton with its long central green comes next. I have already described how the village was relocated by the monks of Jervaulx and the green may have been provided to hold the market, chartered in 1306 but lost after the Black Death ravaged the dale in 1563. (See Chapter 6.)

Two tributary dales join the Ure in this vicinity. Just to the south of Masham there is the junction with the River Burn, which drains the secretive little backwater of Colsterdale. Once the villages of Fearby and Healey have been left behind, the succession of field gates to be opened and closed on the narrow Colsterdale road will deter all but the most determined visitors. Here one feels quite insulated from the clatter and chatter of the modern world. It is strange to imagine that this was an area of medieval industry, the monks of Jervaulx obtaining Colsterdale early in the twelfth century and developing coal and iron mines. In a plantation near the hamlet of Leighton, to the south of the River Burn, is by far the most outlandish monument in this region or most others. Around 1800, William Danby of nearby Swinton provided work for unemployed local labour in the construction of what, to the eyes of any competent prehistorian, is a grotesque parody of a Neolithic temple. Features of Stonehenge and various older megalithic tombs are combined in a 'druidical fantasy' to produce one of Britain's finest yet least known follies. It has no archaeological relevance

but is jolly good fun. Below is the unnatural panorama of Leighton reservoir.

The River Cover joins the Ure to the north of East Witton and from the village a minor road leads to Coverham. Little remains of the abbey, founded here by Ranulph Fitz-Robert early in the thirteenth century, apart from the original Norman gateway and unearthed effigies of two warrior lords of Middleham. The site is now privately owned and viewing is by permission. The Coverdale road leads south-westwards up and over the watershed to Wharfedale via the hamlets of Gammersgill, Horsehouse, Bradley and Woodale. The gentle, verdant countryside gradually yields to stern fells. From the pass at 1600 feet (488 m) the descent into Wharfedale is steep and rapid.

Returning to the main valley at Middleham one encounters one of England's most attractive little castle towns. In this gentle countryside there is nothing more martial than a string of racehorses in training. It is easy to forget that men of the area were mustered by the Fitz-Randolphs and Nevilles of Middleham to engage the armies of the Scottish border barons, or the local claims that during the Wars of the Roses Warwick the Kingmaker could draw 30,000 soldiers and retainers to his banner. The history of Middleham seems to be tied to its castle but the place has older associations. The fourteenth- and fifteenth-century church was dedicated to the Blessed Virgin and St Alkeda, the latter a Saxon noblewoman said to have been martyred here by Danes when she would not renounce her Christian faith. Middleham was an important medieval market centre and the great Middleham Moor Fair, held on 5, 6 and 7 November, endured into the nineteenth century as one of the greatest of the northern fairs. There is a cross in Middleham market square and a second cross, with four steps and two pillars, marking the spot in West End where swine were sold.

Across the Ure from Middleham is Spennithorne, home of Richard Hatfield, a gentleman for whom royalty may have mixed feelings. When a soldier, he is said to have saved the life of the Duke of York yet he attempted to shoot George II at the Drury Lane Theatre. Our road leads across the river to Leyburn, which marks the junction between the gentle, rolling countryside of the middle section of Wensleydale and sterner scenery more characteristic of the Dales. Leyburn is today a major tourist centre of the dale, with roads from all directions converging on its elongated market square. In the past, however, Leyburn was outshone by its neighbours, Middleham and Wensley. Because of its lack of deep and stirring history the treatment of Leyburn in the guide books tends to weave around its nature as an attractive, stone-built townlet. In fact the place was enthusiastically developed by the man who was to become the Duke of Bolton (and whose castle stands a few miles to the west) as a replacement for the failed market centre of Wensley in the seventeenth century.

Wensley lies on the A684 and beside the Ure just to the south-west of Leyburn. Though just a small village today, Wensley can claim what Leyburn lacks in the way of history. The church is several sizes too big for the present village and various pieces of old masonry unearthed in its vicinity – including the carved crosshead preserved in the vestry – tell of an original Saxon foundation. The building which survives is of the twelfth and thirteenth centuries, with fifteenth-century additions. Wensley gained its market charter in 1306 and attached its name to what had previously been Uredale. In 1563 the townlet was struck by the same epidemic of the pestilence which robbed East Witton of its commercial aspirations, and Wensley never recovered. Visiting the place just after the close of the Middle Ages, the chronicler Leland found 'a little poore market toune' and he described partly slated and partly thatched cottages.

On a minor road leading north-west from Wensley is Preston-under-Scar, a village which nestles beneath a scar and which formerly accommodated a mining community. Further along the road is Redmire, seemingly rural and rustic but also once the home of a group of lead and coal miners, whose former workings pockmark Redmire Moor. The outstanding landmark in this area is Castle Bolton, founded by Sir Richard Scrope, Lord Chancellor of England after 1378. Sir Richard obtained a royal permit to crenellate (or fortify) his manor with a wall of stone and lime and then drew up the building contract with one 'John Lewyn, mason', the result being a quadrangular fortress with corner towers which was as much a palace as a castle. The century had gone well for the Scropes and in its earlier decades they purchased the manor of Wensley and exchanged territory to recover land which their forbears had given to Rievaulx Abbey. After the castle was finished a new church was built close by. It is not known whether the village of Castle Bolton, with its neat roadside green, existed before the castle and straddled the old high road or whether it was established by the Scropes as part of their manorial complex. Late in the seventeenth century the family moved to Bolton Hall, near Leyburn. The castle had an active history. In the reign of Elizabeth I her rival, Mary Queen of Scots, was imprisoned here for six months in 1568–9, a prolonged stop in the sad progress of this foolish and ill-fated queen from the vulnerable frontier castle at Carlisle to more secure prisons in the south. She had a suite in the south-west tower and her retinue of some forty members was accommodated in the castle and village. Legend holds that she escaped but was soon recaptured at a spot nearby which is still called 'Queen's Gap'. Fearing that such a dangerous prisoner should not be left in the Catholic north, Elizabeth had her removed to Tutbury Castle in Staffordshire in January 1569. During the Civil War the castle was besieged by Parliamentarians and although it was never designed to withstand an artillery siege it resisted boldly until surrendering on 5 November 1645. Weakened by the

OPPOSITE ABOVE
Wonderful countryside in the Walden area around West Burton

bombardment, the north-west tower fell during a gale in 1761, but otherwise Castle Bolton remains remarkably well preserved.

Returning to the main valley road, we come to West Witton, which lies in the shadow of the 1800-foot (550-m) bulk of Penhill. The village is noted for its custom of burning 'Owd Bartle', for while other villagers burn Guy Fawkes on 5 November, here Bartle is burned on the Saturday closest to St Bartholomew's Day (24 August). The identity of Bartle is something of a mystery. The custom may be a leftover from ancient pagan rites – Bartle may in some way be connected with St Bartholomew, the patron saint of the village, or to a mythical giant living on Penhill. But popular legend regards him as a sheep-stealer who was captured and killed on the hill. When the effigy is burned the locals chant the following doggerel:

> In Penhill Crags he tore his rags
> At Hunter's Thorn he blew his horn
> At Cripplebank Stee he broke his knee
> At Grisgill Beck he broke his neck
> At Wadham's End he couldn't fend
> At Grisgill End he made his end
> Shout lads, shout!

At Bellerby, across the river to the north of Leyburn, there was a cruder custom. A man was tarred and feathered and hauled around the village in a cart while local youths ran around the houses begging for cake and ale.

Aysgarth is reached via the hamlet of Swinithwaite but on the outskirts of the village is the junction with the B6160, which runs up the trough of Bishopdale and over the watershed to enter Wharfedale above Buckden. At the Kidstones Pass the road reaches a height of 1392 feet (424 m). Once the hamlets of Thoralby (formerly noted for its hand-sewn boot industry) and Newbiggin have been left behind the dale has only solitary farmsteads, although it supported a feast and games, which were held in mid-June following the sheep-washing. In early medieval times wolves stalked the dale and it existed as a deer-hunting chase, remaining a royal hunting reserve at the close of the Middle Ages. Close to the Wensleydale end of this road and to the mouth of the lonely valley of the Walden Beck is West Burton, a large village nestling in a place where one might expect no more than a hamlet. West Burton is often described as one of the most picturesque of English villages, but with its large green and lofty spire-shaped cross it seems like a transplant from the softer south. The cross bears the date 1820 but the market which it guarded must have been centuries older and it will have been responsible for the growth of West Burton, which was later sustained by knitting and textiles. The market lapsed long ago but livestock fairs were still being held here in March and May at the start of this century.

OPPOSITE BELOW
West Burton with its green and market cross

On the outskirts of West Burton the Walden Beck cascades across limestone boulders to provide an introduction to the falls so characteristic of Wensleydale. The best-known example is Aysgarth Falls on the Ure below Aysgarth village. They are not one falls but three, with the Ure tumbling over a series of limestone terraces in a turbulent stretch more than half a mile in length. After glaciation scoured the valley floor smooth, the river nibbled away at the softer bands of black shale within the limestone beds, which present a series of steps as they dip gently upstream. Fossil scallop shells and corals can be seen in some of the rocks. Near to the road bridge is a crafts centre occupying a mill whose predecessor was built for cotton manufacture in 1784. The surviving mill building was built as a woollen mill in 1853 and later switched to flour milling. In the summer the Ure is low and it is far better to see the Aysgarth Falls out of season when the water thunders and the distractions are gone.

The parish church at Aysgarth originally served a gigantic parish of more than 80,000 acres (32,375 ha) and was the destination of many corpse roads. It was built in Norman times, redeveloped in the thirteenth century and then refurbished by the last Abbot of Jervaulx, while at the time of the dissolution the carved timberwork of the rood screen and loft was brought here from Jervaulx. However, most of the external appearance of the church is the result of a nineteenth-century restoration. The village of Aysgarth, to the east of the church, has a potter's shop and workshop, where a distinctive tableware with a buff base and simple decoration in pastel pink, blue, yellow and green is produced.

Across the river from Aysgarth is Carperby. This is yet another of Wensleydale's old market centres. The cross, standing on what was a tiny triangular green, bears the date 1634. More recently the village is noted for winning 'best-kept village' competitions – a sure sign of forbearance on behalf of the locals, for whenever I see such judges with their clipboards my first instinct is to throw a brick. This forbearance was less evident to the guidebook writer, Edmund Bogg, who was here a century ago:

> Whilst passing through this place we met one or two of the most rustic figures, whose artistic outlines blended in such perfect unison into the surroundings, enough to cause the soul of any true artist to leap with joy. In the hurricane of wind and rain which was then passing, we had some difficulty to persuade the principal figure to stand until we obtained a sketch, in fact, words were of no avail, it was only the sight of money that won the day.*

Further up the valley Askrigg and Bainbridge face each other across the river. On the eastern outskirts of Askrigg stands Nappa Hall; it lies close to

*'From Edenvale to the Plains of York: OR, A Thousand Miles in the Valleys of The Nidd and Yore', c. 1900, John Sampson, Coney Street, York. See Bibliography.

the road entering Askrigg from the west but, as it is in private occupation and serves as a farmhouse and guest house, it is more considerate to view it from the road on the south side of the river. This also gives a much more comprehensive view. Nappa Hall is a fine example of a pele tower, a fortified dwelling created to provide a family of substance with protection against Scottish raiding parties. The house had a characteristic medieval plan with a long hall bracketed by cross wings at either end. Each wing rose to form a tower, the west tower being much the larger, thick-walled and four storeys tall. It was built between 1450 and 1459 by Thomas Metcalfe, who fought at Agincourt and 'waxed rich and builded . . . two faire towers'. The Metcalfes were hard men who served as estate stewards for the abbots of Jervaulx and for the king as wardens of the Forest of Wensleydale. They played a leading role in defending the north against Scottish invasion and developed strong bonds of trust with their more powerful neighbours, the Scropes of Castle Bolton and the Nevilles of Middleham. Their arms, three black calves on a silver shield, relate to a family legend which claims, most improbably, that the founder of the dynasty, a Saxon named Oswald, went out into the forest to confront a lion but met only a red calf instead. Even less credible is the myth that the founder of the dynasty was a man named Armstrong who was knighted and changed his name in 1312 after he had felled a runaway bull with a single blow at royal fête in Chelmsford. In 1556 Sir Christopher Metcalfe, the High Sheriff of Yorkshire, flaunted his power by meeting the judges of assize at York at the head of a retinue of 300 Metcalfes, all mounted on white horses. Members of the family certainly did their best to populate the dale and the surname is still extremely common hereabouts. At the end of the Middle Ages the family was said to be the largest in England, perhaps due in part to a genetic tendency to produce male heirs. Today it has its own annual gathering and its own society – features more like those of the Scottish clans with which the old Metcalfes fought. Metcalfes lived in Nappa Hall until 1756 but the ghost said to haunt the house is not a Metcalfe but that of Mary Queen of Scots, a guest at the hall during her incarceration.

Askrigg was a medieval settlement with a church which served as a chapel of ease for Aysgarth. The original church of 1175 was rebuilt in 1240, and gained a tower in the fifteenth century and further additions in the sixteenth century. Church and churchyard stand in the heart of the townlet, flanked by terraced cottages and shops. There may have been no medieval market charter, for to 'lighten the grievous journeys and labours' faced by villagers bound for 'other markets very remote', Queen Elizabeth granted Askrigg a market and two fairs in 1587. (Askrigg Hill Fair seems to have provided the main venue for brawls between the male contingents of Wensleydale and Swaledale.) This commercial advantage lasted for only a century, for in 1699 Hawes, further up the dale, gained its own market

Wensleydale

charter and Askrigg's role as a trading centre declined; the market lapsed at the beginning of the nineteenth century. Instead the people turned to industry and behind the façade of tall buildings flanking the main street were the dwellings of spinners, dyers and lead-miners. Hand-knitting was very important and a seventeenth-century visitor, 'Drunken Barnaby', asserted that 'here poor people live by knitting; to their trading, breeding, sitting'. Askrigg gained a cotton mill in 1784 which converted into a woollen mill producing yarn for the local hand-knitters. The hand-knitting trade was still alive in Askrigg a century ago. Another more specialised trade which developed here was clock-making, and clocks bearing the names of Askrigg clock-makers Christopher Caygill, Mark Metcalfe and James Ogden are collectors' items.

If Askrigg seems vaguely familiar to the first-time visitor this is not a case of *déjà-vu*, for Askrigg contains the building used as 'Skeldale House' in the Herriot television programmes. In consequence it is now a magnet for day-trippers. I do not know whether fell racing is partly derived from an old Askrigg custom, but on St Oswald's Day, 16 August, a race up a steep hill to the north of the village was formerly held, the winner receiving a large woven garland. Legend holds that the race was instituted centuries ago as a punishment for the men of Wensleydale by a lady unlucky in love. She was

OPPOSITE ABOVE
Nappa Hall

OPPOSITE BELOW
The medieval church at Askrigg

The bridge and beck in the middle of Hawes

said to have endowed the parish with a field, the rents from which paid for the village saint's-day feast.

Returning to the south side of the river, Bainbridge stands at the mouth of the deep valley of the River Bain, a valley which broadens to accommodate the glacial lake of Semer Water, beyond which is lovely Raydale, drained by the Raydale Beck. The scene is dominated by the bulk of Addlebrough, not the loftiest of fells but one with a more noble profile than most and a commanding presence over the best part of Wensleydale. Like its eastern neighbour, Pen Hill, it preserves traces of prehistoric fields and dwellings on its high flanks. As we have seen, there are the faint remains of the Roman camp of Virosidum on the glacial mound overlooking Bainbridge, while the village is said to have been founded before 1228 to house a community of twelve foresters by the lords of Middleham. A relic of Bainbridge's forest past survived in the custom of sounding the forest horn every night at ten o'clock from the feast of the Holy Rood in late September to Shrovetide – this to beckon lost travellers benighted in the (long-departed) woods. The horn used once adorned an African buffalo and replaced an earlier horn in 1864; it is kept in the Rose and Crown Inn. The village has both a large green and a predominantly green road, the latter a track developed by the Romans as part of their policing system, and running south-westwards to Ribblehead and Ingleton.

Semer Water is the remainder of a larger lake and a reminder of times when glacial lakes and marshes covered the floors of all the dales. It has an area of about 90 acres (36 ha) and, at times when the power-boaters are not spoiling things for everyone else, it is a place of beauty and tranquillity. By the lakeshore is the Carlow Stone, a great boulder dumped by the waning ice. The remains of prehistoric lake-dwellings have been found here but Semer Water is better known for the legend of a submerged city. This claims that in early Christian times a pauper wandered into this rich and fair city to beg for food. He was denied and evicted but was given food and shelter by a humble couple living beyond the city bounds. The next day he raised his hand and placed a curse on the city below, and the stream swelled to become a lake which engulfed all the streets and dwellings. Former generations of Bainbridge dwellers would insist that the roofs of the dwellings could be seen beneath the waters of Semer Water. Close to the lake shore is Countersett, where Countersett Hall was the home of George Fox, the founder of Quakerism. There could have been few better places to formulate high principles or savour the value of silence – Fox did not have power-boats to contend with.

Four miles further up the dale from Askrigg is Hawes. We are now deep in upland country and it seems surprising to discover so vibrant a townlet. There were medieval hamlets here and a chapel was established in the late fifteenth century – though the church tower is of the nineteenth century.

The rise of Hawes can be dated to 1699 when a market charter was received from William III and Hawes proceeded to capture the trade of Askrigg. This advantage was underlined almost a century later when an improved toll road or turnpike was built to Lancaster, allowing wheeled transport to compete with the pack-horse teams. Meanwhile Hawes and the adjacent hamlets of Gayle and Burtersett developed quarries and textile mills, and the old hand-knitting industry continued to flourish. The lively trade allowed a Market Hall to be built in 1902 and the Tuesday market remains a flourishing affair. Writing a century ago, Edmund Bogg told his readers that, while Leyburn, Redmire, Aysgarth and Askrigg were developing their tourist trades, at Hawes 'the business of the countryside seems the first and only consideration, for at present small effort is made to attract visitors'. The charge could scarcely be levelled at Hawes today for there is a National Park information centre, folk museum and cheese- and pottery-making. Mr Bogg described the bustle of the market, where a wine merchant offered bottles of sherry and port at 6s (30p) per dozen, but complained of loungers on the bridge at Gayle nearby who were lulled to sleep by the murmuring of the beck. The Gayle Beck bisects both Gayle and Hawes and creates scenes of memorable beauty in both places. The two villages also lie on the route of the Pennine Way and Hawes has a large youth hostel with accommodation for sixty.

Almost opposite Hawes on the north side of the Ure is the hamlet of Hardraw and the 98-foot (30-m) high waterfall of Hardraw Force. Here the shaft of water falls unimpeded from the brow of an undercut cliff. It is reached via the bar of the Green Dragon Inn and a pleasant footpath along the beck.

From Hawes roads lead to Ingleton, Sedbergh and Kirkby Stephen but the fell country drained by the headwaters of the Ure remain bleak and largely deserted. This is the lonely birthplace of the Rivers Ure, Swale and Eden. Looking back on the lower reaches of the dale we see a broad, flat-floored corridor which is relatively rich in farming resources and richer in history. While perhaps lacking the intensities of beauty of the more rugged and uncompromising dale to the north, Wensleydale offers rather more for the car-borne family party out to enjoy a day – or a week – in the country.

CHAPTER 16

Nidderdale

Until quite recently Nidderdale could have been described as 'the forgotten dale', but this is no longer so. However it can be characterised emphatically as the dale of lost opportunity. The dale contains several reservoirs and it is said that water interests were responsible for the unpardonable mistake of excluding it from the Yorkshire Dales National Park. An awful price has been paid for this exclusion, including the disfigurement of more than one lovely village. There are connoisseurs of the dales who regard Nidderdale as the finest dale of all, and whether or not one agrees with this there is no arguing with the fact that the lusher, darker gritstone scenery of Nidderdale should have been included to complement and contrast with the limestone dales.

Harrogate stands on the doorstep of the dale and at nearby Knaresborough the Nidd has carved a gorge of truly dramatic proportions. It is therefore surprising that no riverside road is available until one has travelled a few miles into the dale. Visitors from Knaresborough or Harrogate encounter the River Nidd between Ripley and Killinghall, where a fine sixteenth-century bridge has been sidestepped by a modern river crossing on the A61. Killinghall, a village which migrated across its former common to take up a position beside a new turnpike at the end of the eighteenth century, has little to attract the visitor apart from an exceptionally good plant nursery, but Ripley, across the river, is quite different. Legend tells that Ripley was granted to the Ingilby family after Thomas Ingilby saved Edward III from mutilation by a charging boar in 1347 (another version holds that the event took place in Norman times and that the knight was rewarded with the gift of Haverah Park, near Harrogate). In 1357 Ripley gained a market and fair, and an unusually fine cross and stocks survive in the cobbled village square. In due course the lords of the manor fortified their house, remains of which include a fifteenth-century gatehouse and a

Hampsthwaite churchyard

tower of 1555. The attractive church is said to be a replacement for one undermined by the Nidd at the end of the fourteenth century, although the clerestory and upper tower are of the sixteenth century. In the churchyard there is a rare example of a very old penitential or weeping cross. The shaft has gone but the grooves in the base for the knees of the penitents are well preserved.

The Ingilby family remained loyal to the Roman Catholic cause after the tide of politics favoured the Protestant faith. After the Battle of Marston Moor, Cromwell billeted his troops in the village and himself in the castle, much to the distress of Mistress Ingilby, who later proclaimed her readiness to shoot him. Bullet scars in the church wall are believed to commemorate the execution of Royalist prisoners here. Sir William Ingilby supported Guy Fawkes and is said to have escaped execution by bribing the prosecution witness. In 1963 a priest-hole was discovered behind the wainscotting in the castle and will have been used to secrete the priests who celebrated the Mass here during the years of religious persecution.

At the start of the nineteenth century Ripley was a village of shabby thatched hovels like many others in the neighbourhood. In the 1820s, however, it was completely transformed by Sir William Amcotts Ingilby who replaced the old dwellings with splendid stone houses and terraces in a mock-Elizabethan style. Then in 1854 Lady Amcotts Ingilby provided Ripley with a French *hôtel de ville*; it is a bizarre addition and one might well imagine that the villagers would rather have gained an inn. But affairs in Ripley were strictly regulated. There was also a rule that only one representative of each trade could operate here.

Seen at its best Ripley is an absolutely delightful place but its face has been its misfortune. Day-trippers are augmented by visitors linked with the various commercial activities associated with the castle and park, and in summer Ripley can be so submerged by strangers that one feels a deep sympathy for residents, who lack front gardens to provide a *cordon sanitaire* between their living rooms and the throng. The memorable scenes of cross, church, market square and mock-Elizabethan dwellings in this 'village of vision' are best enjoyed in winter.

A couple of miles upstream and across the river is Hampsthwaite. If Ripley's face is its misfortune, Hampsthwaite's misfortune lies at the other end – a great rump of suburban housing development which has over-whelmed and transformed this pleasant village. Yet, with a little care, one can still detect the traditional form of the village – a long street running down to a riverside church and crossing at the place where the Roman road from Ilkley to Aldborough traversed the Nidd. Near the middle of the old village road there is a broadening with a triangular green, which was most probably created around 1304, when Hampsthwaite gained its fair and market charter. This was a royal village lying like most of the land to the south of the Nidd in the King's Forest of Knaresborough and in medieval times through to Georgian times it specialised in the manufacture of spurs, which were sold at Ripon market. The medieval church has an unusual dedication to Thomas à Becket; it contains the extravagant tomb of Amy Woodforde-Finden, composer of the 'Indian Love Lyrics' and in the graveyard lies local-boy-made-good William Makepeace Thackeray. Not all local boys made good and early in the nineteenth century Hampsthwaite residents and parsons alike had a reputation for brawling, betting, cursing and other vices. Beside the church is a handsome seventeenth-century stone bridge, the successor to a sequence of timber bridges carried away by the floods of the Nidd. Now the threat comes not from floods but from juggernauts; the side of the bridge has been repaired after its last encounter with one of the giant trucks which plague the lanes hereabouts. The part of the village between the green and the church has been made a conservation area and here one can recall how pleasant old Hampsthwaite really was before it fell a victim to 'progress'.

The road leading over Hampsthwaite bridge was for centuries the main thoroughfare between York and Lancaster. When the old route branches off to become a narrow lane, now incorporated into the 'Nidderdale Way' footpath, one realises just how crude the old roads were. Until the 1860s a pub known as the Lamb in Hampsthwaite was used by pack-horse traders working between York and Skipton and it had stabling for the ponies. Our road curves around to bring us to Clint on the crest of a ridge overlooking the valley. At first glance Clint seems to be composed of a line of unexciting early-twentieth-century houses, but these dwellings stand on the site of the deserted medieval and Elizabethan village inhabited by makers of spurs and spinners and weavers of wool and flax. The main clue stands right at the roadside – the old village cross base and stocks. Carved on the cross are the words 'Palliser the tailor', chipped into the stone by a Knaresborough draper who left several advertisements of this kind. At the other end of Clint are the isolated ruins of the late-medieval hall of the Beckwith family.

Next up the valley is Birstwith. In 1871 the historian William Grainge declared, 'this is the most beautiful and best cultivated district within the Forest of Knaresborough'. In 1906 another local historian, Harry Speight, found the position of Birstwith 'strikingly picturesque. Wood and water and luxuriant pasture – lands, pleasant county houses with posied gardens are everywhere around.' And a few years earlier Edmund Bogg considered the village 'clean, well-built and healthy, and an air of comfort pervades the homes of the peasants, which stand in well-kept gardens adjoining the roadway, which rises to the beautiful church standing on a well-wooded slope'. Writers also praised the oak trees, which still grow so splendidly in the parish. One might deduce from all this praise that this was a mellow and ancient village, but not at all, for when these words were written Birstwith was still in its infancy. It was the creation of the Greenwood family, who had made a fortune from their cotton mills at Keighley. John Greenwood bought an old house at Birstwith, known as Swarcliffe Hall, in 1805 and gained control of a new cotton mill established on the riverside below. In the course of the century which followed, the Greenwoods bought up most of the land in the parish, enlarged their house until it became a stately home, built estate housing, a church – widely praised but with a broach spire more characteristic of Northamptonshire than of Yorkshire – a school and a reading room.

Birstwith exists as a splendid and, in several vistas, beautiful example of landscape and architecture created by Victorian patronage. The legacy survives largely intact in the area around the church and village shop and post office, although a lovely feature known as the 'plantpot', a round stone-walled enclosure containing mature trees, has been lost to official vandalism and degraded in stages to the tedious roundabout existing now. A local conservation group recently proposed the creation of a conservation area to encompass the old Greenwood legacy of village landscape, but officialdom was not impressed and the future of this special corner of village England remains uncertain. A road leads down to the fine three-arch

*The former hall of the
Greenwood family,
church, vicarage and
man-made falls at
Birstwith*

Georgian bridge, but to reach it one must pass what many locals and visitors
alike regard as one of the very worst of modern eyesores in the Dales – the
vast metal sheds of the food-ingredients mill which were erected during the
1980s by the giant Dalgety conglomerate. The clash between these
featureless curtain walls and the setting of woods, parkland, oak and
riverside alder could scarcely jar more.

The theme of latterday barbarism is unfortunately resumed at Darley, the
next village up the valley. The modern visitor, most probably little
bothered to see the back of Darley, could scarcely imagine that even in the
1950s this was one of the prettiest of all the villages in the Dales. Old maps
and the disposition of the old buildings in Darley show that it existed as
clusters of cottages and farmsteads set around the edges of several small
greens. On one surviving green the old village stocks still stand. Sadly the
presence of greens and the gaps between them proved irresistible to
developers and Darley's special charms counted for nothing. So now the
buildings of old Darley stand embedded in a jumbled morass of modern

Pateley Bridge

building. Most recently the elders of Darley have appealed for more low-cost housing in the village – but it scarcely matters any more.

The worst of the mindless modern development which has so devalued the villages of this lovely dale ends – at present – at Darley. Just beyond Darley there is a symbol of how commerce and conservation can flourish together. A large old mill has recently been converted into a linen and craft goods store and tea rooms. External and internal features have been thoughtfully preserved and the great waterwheel restored. Extending far and wide around the mill is an exceptionally fine landscape produced by the parliamentary enclosure of the Forest of Knaresborough in the late eighteenth century. The straight stone walls create geometrical patterns to produce a sequence of remarkable fieldscapes.

The first zone of Nidderdale is characterised by captivating villages, each in some way spoiled by modern values. The next zone, culminating at the old market centre of Pateley Bridge, is one of hidden industry. Hamlets and villages occur at frequent intervals and between and among them are the remains of old leets, races and mill dams, all a legacy of the days of water-powered industry. In 1818 there were some forty mills in the valley, most associated with the spinning, weaving and bleaching of linen. At Summerbridge flax and hemp were worked at the New York Mills for around a century and mills such as this sucked in the older cottage flax-spinning industries. Another old flax-mill lay across the river in Dacre Banks. Further up the valley there are the hamlets of Wilsill and Braisty Woods, which once had tanning industries, Smelthouses, where Fountains Abbey had a smelter for lead ore brought down from Greenhow and which later gained a flax-mill, and Glasshouses, which also had a flax-mill.

Just to the north-east of this formerly industrial section of the valley is Brimham Rocks, a splendid vantage point which is famous for its weirdly sculpted gritstone tors. The scenery is so similar to that of the Dartmoor granite that in 1988 Granada Television filmed the Sherlock Holmes story *The Hound of the Baskervilles* here. Brimham was a grange of Fountains Abbey and later this eminence was chosen as the site for a warning beacon. Until around a century ago people believed that spirits inhabited the rocks. As a boy I would cycle here and enjoy scenery that was wild but serene, looking far across the Vale of York to the towers of York Minister or westwards across the woods and geometrical fieldscape of Nidderdale. The rocks were owned by a rather eccentric local character, and efforts to collect tolls were cursory. Now Brimham Rocks is owned by the National Trust and the serenity has gone, at least in summer. In winter, and particularly in the snow, a visit here is still well worthwhile.

All roads hereabouts lead to Pateley Bridge, which I described in Chapter 9. The town receives many visitors, the tourist trade being well established by early June when the tradespeople put out the hanging flower-baskets for which Pateley Bridge is renowned. Only a tiny minority of visitors know of or attempt the steep walk to the old church, though the ruins are as romantic as any in the Dales and the churchyard, for those of a morbid disposition, contains the graves of quadruplets born in 1755 and of Mary Myers, who died in 1743 at the age of almost 120 years. Just across the river is Bewerley, once the focus of a vast manor which included Grassington in Wharfedale and which was granted by the mighty Roger de Mowbray to Fountains Abbey in the twelfth century. Fine panoramas of Pateley Bridge and its setting can be seen from the minor roads to Kirkby Malzeard or Heyshaw Moor, but most visitors arriving from the south-east will either cross the moors and watershed and enter Wharfedale or else continue up the valley into upper Nidderdale. The B6265 bound for Grassington makes a very steep ascent of the valley side to reach Greenhow Hill, situated at a height of around 1300 feet (395 m) and one of the loftiest villages in England. Not so long ago Greenhow Hill seemed to be a terminal victim of the collapse of lead-mining in the Pennines, but during the 1980s the sale and refurbishment of the estate cottages here has repopulated the village. A little further along the road are the Stump Cross Caverns, lying just on the Wharfedale side of the watershed in a bleak landscape ripped and pockmarked by the frenzied scrabblings of t'owd man. Discovered by two of the last of the lead-miners in 1860, the caverns have a good associated display area.

Upper Nidderdale is quite distinctive and much more rural and remote in character than the section of the dale lying below Pateley Bridge. The villages here are descended from medieval granges, the territory having been divided between the abbeys of Fountains and Byland. The industrial zone of Nidderdale is not quite left behind, for a little upstream from Pateley Bridge there is the mid-nineteenth-century Foster Beck mill which made heavy yarns and retains its great 35-foot (11-m) high breast waterwheel, which was installed in 1904. It survived as a spinning-mill until 1966 and is now an inn. A little further upstream the valley floor lies beneath Gouthwaite reservoir, which was built between 1893 and 1901 to provide water for Bradford and which exploits a glacial moraine barrier so that the amount of artificial dam construction is minimised. The building of Gouthwaite reservoir greatly tamed the Nidd and the regulation of the river has eliminated the troublesome floods of earlier times. With a storage capacity of 1.5 billion gallons (7 billion litres), it cost just £100,000. This is a favourite spot for bird-watchers, who are excluded from the shore of the reservoir and restricted to roadside vantage points. The most interesting birds are seen when the water level is down and marshes fringe the shoreline.

At the upper end of the reservoir lies the hamlet of Ramsgill. This was a grange of Byland Abbey, while Bouthwaite and Covill nearby were granges of Fountains Abbey. In the churchyard there are the remains of the monastic chapel; much more of this interesting building survived until 1842 when an idiotic demolition coincided with the building of the church. In the course of the nineteenth century Ramsgill seems to have withered, for around 1900 the oldest locals reported that they could remember at least a score of thatched homesteads being abandoned over the years. The pub was rebuilt in 1843 and its name, the Yorke Arms, commemorates the dynasty which commanded great power in upper Nidderdale. Lofthouse comes next, and this was a grange of Fountains Abbey. Local legend claims that the little village gained its name when an old farmhouse of about 1650 standing opposite the Crown Hotel had a loft or upper storey added – but the name can be traced back to earlier centuries. Even so it is worth noting that elsewhere in the Dales 'loft-houses' were mentioned in the decades around 1600; they were dwellings in which boards were placed above the tie beams linking the crucks of the timber upper storey or loft.

From Lofthouse a narrow road coinciding with an old market track can be

ABOVE LEFT
One of the weird outcrops at Brimham Rocks

ABOVE RIGHT
The How Stean Gorge in Nidderdale

followed across the wild grouse moors to Masham. This is an attractive route, but before taking it one should try to visit the lovely How Stean Gorge, just west of the Lofthouse–Middlesmoor road. Here the How Stean Beck discovered a narrow band of limestone among the surrounding grits and exploited the yielding rock to gouge a deep gorge. The walls of the gorge, which fall sheer for more than 30 feet (9 m) in places, are fringed with plants, and shafts of sunlight pierce the tree canopy to lighten the depths of the trough. There are narrow bridges and slippery paths and a good pair of shoes and a sense of balance are advised. Just south of Lofthouse the Nidd emerges – or re-emerges – at Nidd Heads, the main river having flowed underground in a limestone labyrinth for about 2 miles (3.2 km). The course of a former railway built to transport materials during the construction of Scar House reservoir now forms a private road to the reservoir which is open to visitors. Near a picnic area by the road is the entrance to Goyden Pot, a cavern into which the river flows at times of high water. It should never be entered, even if the smallest stream is flowing in, for a torrent of water could follow.

Middlesmoor is the last village in the dale and one of the loveliest in all the region. It has a proud hillside position and the village and church seem particularly noble when seen from Lofthouse or the How Stean locality. The view of Nidderdale looking down from Middlesmoor churchyard is even grander. In medieval times this was a property of Byland Abbey and part of the gigantic 53,000-acre (21,450-ha) parish of Kirby Malzeard. Until 1484 both corpses for burial and babies for christening had to be taken along rough tracks to Kirby, a journey of more than 10 miles (16 km). In this year a chapel was sanctioned for Middlesmoor and this church was almost completely rebuilt in 1865–6. However, the presence here of an ancient preaching cross suggests that Christianity was established in this enchanting place at a very early date. After its monastic beginnings Middlesmoor developed as a village of agricultural workers, quarrymen and miners, the stone cottages forming attractively informal rows and clusters. In those days of innocence before the creation of the greenhouse effect this

The hilltop church at Middlesmoor

locality was known for the severity of its snowfalls and in November 1904 houses in the village were buried by drifts up to their eaves.

Unlike the other major dales, Nidderdale is a cul-de-sac. The old pack-horse track from Middlesmoor to Wharfedale no longer exists, although ramblers can cross Arkleside Moor to Coverdale. At the head of the dale are the Angram and Scar House reservoirs, built for Bradford Corporation between 1904 and 1936. Some visitors drive up via Lofthouse and park close to the reservoirs, though the scenery is far too unnatural for my taste and the man-made lakes an unwelcome reminder of the forces which excluded the dale from the National Park. Currently there are plans afoot to make upper Nidderdale an Area of Outstanding Natural Beauty – which, of course, it has always been. The elders in the affected areas (almost entirely farmers) are objecting on the grounds that this designation would attract visitors. While one can sympathise with anyone who does not want to lose the priceless gift of tranquillity, one cannot help thinking it rather churlish of farmers to grab public subsidies by the handful yet grumble and gripe when their benefactors come too close.

The headwaters of the Nidd are embraced by the fells of Great and Little Whernside and Meugher, with Great Whernside rising to 2310 feet (704 m). Here there is also Dead Man's Hill, where in 1728 three headless bodies, thought to be those of murdered Scottish tinkers, were unearthed from the peat. These facts are known because the costs of the inquest and burial are recorded in the old township books for Middlesmoor. However, a more creative version of the legend tells of the keepers of a lonely inn on the Masham–Kettlewell track who disposed of some twenty-five customers, stole their money and released their horses on the moor. Not worth many stars in the AA handbook of the time, one assumes.

CHAPTER 17

Wharfedale and the Craven Dales

Wharfedale is a dale of contrasts. One cannot distil the essence of the scenery in any one sweeping panorama, but rather the image is that of a mosaic or collage of scenes. In the course of a few miles one may see three or four quite different countrysides, the wooded, the rugged, the verdant and the bleak, each one entirely delightful and self-contained. While the other great dales have their heads in the windy fells and their feet in the placid vale, Wharfedale's rural bliss is cut short, for its knees lie in the margins of the Leeds–Bradford conurbation.

We have already glanced at the Wharfedale market towns of Otley and Ilkley, but the dale does not assume its wholly rural character until the southern boundary of the National Park is reached just south of Bolton Bridge. First, however, a tributary valley between the dales of the Wharfe and the Nidd should not be overlooked – the Washburn valley, now partly drowned by the reservoirs of Fewston, Swinsty and Thruscross. The valley was punctuated with flax-mills, of which only the Low Mill at West End was still working at the start of this century; now West End itself is drowned by Thruscross reservoir. Previously the valley floor was patterned with a close succession of ponds, dams and leets and nine great waterwheels turned in the vicinity of West End, two of them giants of 40 feet (12 m) diameter. The West House mill was particularly notorious for the cruel exploitation of child labour. Up to 200 infants were housed in two 'Prentice Houses' and they worked from 6 a.m. until 8 p.m. or later, many having their feet and legs permanently deformed through standing at the machines. Few tears were shed when the mills closed around 1870.

A few years later work was completed on the Leeds Corporation reservoirs of Fewston and Swinsty. The old village of Fewston partly collapsed in a landslide as the waters of Swinsty reservoir were sucked into its foundations of shale and gravel, and until the ruins were demolished they attracted frequent parties of visitors from Harrogate. Thruscross reservoir was built further up the valley in the 1960s and the failed and shrunken mill village was completely depopulated, a few former inhabitants returning to the setting of their earlier lives during the droughts of the mid-1970s and 1989. Beneath the reservoir near Fewston is Newhall, home between 1600 and 1635 of Edward Fairfax, a recluse who published a remarkable tirade against witchcraft around 1621. He accused a local coven of half a dozen witches of casting spells upon his daughters and of inducing local people to burn calves alive. Twice he had women tried for witchcraft at York assizes but fortunately they were acquitted. On the moors just to the west are several rocks carved with prehistoric cup-and-ring marks.

Returning to the main valley there is a zone of concentrated interest beginning with the genuinely romantic ruins of Bolton Priory. Actually there is rather more than ruins; the Augustinians involved local people in their affairs and after the dissolution the nave of the monastic church was preserved for lay worship, a role which it performs to this day. Nearby the arch of an eighteenth-century mill aqueduct spans and narrows the B6160,

The Wharfe at Bolton Priory

providing a welcome restriction on the size of vehicles which can penetrate further up the dale. Beside the road an old monastic gatehouse was converted into a shooting lodge for the dukes of Devonshire, who own much grouse moor hereabouts and numbered British kings and prime ministers among their guests. A little further along is the ornate fountain erected as a monument to Lord Frederick Cavendish, who was brutally murdered in Phoenix Park.

Here a private road runs down to the riverside and Strid Woods. Nature lovers may be put off by the ranks of cars and the large cafeteria but in fact the crowds soon melt away as one enters the woods and long walks are available on both sides of the river. This is not natural woodland for beech, larch and other more exotic trees have been introduced into the estate woodland. Nonetheless it is woodland of considerable natural importance and is noted for the autumn eruptions of fungus. Deep in the woods is the Strid, where the Wharfe is constricted and shoots into a narrow chasm. From time to time visitors believe they can jump the Strid. They are usually right, but fail to realise that the slope of the landing is such as to throw one back into torrents which can be more than 25 feet (8 m) deep. The floor is gouged by whirlpools so that the waters pump and twist, and there is no

BELOW LEFT
The dangerous Strid

BELOW
Falls in the Valley of Desolation

record of anyone failing to jump the Strid more than once. One of my own favourite walks follows the Valley of Desolation, reached by crossing the Wharfe at the cafeteria, bearing upstream and then following the footpath across the old deer park of the Prior of Bolton. Otherwise known as the Possforth Gill, the Valley of Desolation received its more colourful name after a severe storm and cloudburst spawned a flood which swept away all the trees early in the nineteenth century. Today this damage is no longer evident and the wonderful waterfalls, woods, bracken and colours which often seem more intense than elsewhere make this anything but a valley of desolation.

The Barden Tower, which stands at the roadside just upstream of Strid Woods, is an important landmark. An old hunting lodge in the Clifford game reserve was enlarged by Henry Clifford in 1485, fell into ruin about a century later and was restored by that human dynamo, Lady Anne Clifford, in 1658. Now, unpretentious, home-made meals of high quality and modest price are served in the genuinely old interior of the priest house just beside the ruined tower. (Mrs Bootham's speciality – hotpot – is to be recommended!) A little way up the road is a gallery and craft store which generally displays paintings and etchings of real originality as well as the workmanlike but repetitive Dales subjects so widely available elsewhere. Close to Barden Tower is a handsome bridge built by a levy on the county of West Yorkshire in 1676 following the destruction of its predecessor – and several other Wharfedale bridges – in a great flood three years earlier. The narrow road which crosses this bridge can be followed to the prettily named hamlet of Appletreewick, a medieval grange of Bolton Priory which contains three old halls, one of them the Monk's Hall. Early in the seventeenth century hunting rights around Appletreewick, in what was still a wild and desolate locality, were disputed between two great Dales families, the Yorkes and the Cliffords, and this culminated in a minor battle in which the Skipton contingent was routed by the servants of Sir Thomas Yorke, this gentleman being fined £200 by the Star Chamber as a consequence. A couple of miles to the north-east of Appletreewick are the mansion and gardens of Parceval Hall, an Elizabethan mansion reputed to have harboured a notorious highwayman, William Nevison. This noble farmhouse now serves as a diocesan retreat and conference centre, and the gardens are open to the public.

Near the gates to the hall there is a footpath which can be followed up Trollers Gill and into a narrow limestone gorge. This is the haunt of the mythical 'barguest', a spectral hound said to be huge, black, gaunt and shaggy with eyes like balls of fire. It was reputed to be harmless when left alone, but murderous to those, like the drunken John Lambert from near Skyrethornes and one of the barguest's various victims, who attempted to do battle with it. It cannot be denied that, were one to be a ghostly black dog, then Trollers Gill is the sort of place where one could feel quite at home.

Returning to the Wharfe at Burnsall, we encounter one of the dale's most historic villages. Close to the village are the holy wells of St Margaret and St Helen while inside the church are Dark Age cross fragments, a Viking hogback tomb, and a Norman font, all indicative of a deeply established tradition of worship. The fine church, with its work from several medieval centuries, was restored by a lord mayor of London, Sir William Craven, in 1612. His family were yeomen in the Appletreewick district, but a third son, William, chose to seek his fortune in London and worked for a silk-mercer before establishing his own business and laying the foundations of a new dynasty, the earls of Craven. Known as the 'Dick Whittington of the Dales', Sir William founded a grammar school beside Burnsall church and restored the village bridge. Sadly the bridge had to be replaced in the 1880s and the church suffered at the hands of restorers in 1859. Burnsall is noted for the sports held in mid-August and the fell race is one of the oldest, dating from around 1850. Exceptionally fine views of the village and its lovely riverside setting can be enjoyed from the little Burnsall–Hebden road.

Above Burnsall the scenery becomes more rugged. Grassington stands on the eastern side of the Wharfe and has been a local trading centre since 1282, when the lord of the manor, Roger de Plumpton, paid the King £10 for the right to hold a weekly market and a fair around the Feast of St Michael and All Saints – 28–30 September. The monks did not gain control of Grassington, but the village lay on the busy route between the western estates and the grange at Kilnsey and Fountains Abbey. In 1190 Nigel de Plumpton gave the monks and abbey servants a right to passage across his lands provided that they avoided the grain and meadow land. During the fifteenth century, if not before, lead was mined on Lea Green above the village in a setting patterned by the relics of Iron Age and Roman farming. In the seventeenth and eighteenth centuries the mining activities became more purposeful and since their decline around a century ago the old spoil heaps have been scoured for the valuable minerals barytes and fluorspar. At the peak of the lead industry around 1850 the Cupola smelt-mill discharged its poisons into the Pennine air and 140 Grassington men were employed in mining and processing work. There was also employment in worsted mills in Grassington and across the river in Linton, but the decline in both sources of employment during the second half of the nineteenth century saw the population of the village plummet from 1138 in 1851 to just 480 in 1901. Grassington is an extremely picturesque village and was even more attractive before 1965, when the Main Street lost its cobbles, though the square was recobbled in 1973. It is also an extremely popular centre for visitors, so even in the depths of winter it seems

The Barden Tower

impossible to discover just how delightful the lanes and square would be without the clutter of cars.

On the western outskirts of Grassington is Grass Wood, a wood of great botanical importance which boasts more than 300 varieties of plants. Here Tom Lee, the village blacksmith, murdered the local doctor, Richard Petty, and threw the body into the Wharfe. He was tried for the murder on no less than three separate occasions but was twice found 'not guilty'. At the third trial Lee's apprentice turned King's Evidence and the blacksmith was hanged at the entrance to Grass Wood in 1768.

Though greatly modified, Grassington Bridge is the oldest surviving bridge on the upper Wharfe and dates from 1604. Across the bridge is the aggressively modern Roman Catholic church at Threshfield, of which the least said about the architecture the better. By the river just to the east is the beautiful little village of Linton with its falls, stepping stones and fine church, one of the oldest in the Dales.

The scenery becomes more delightful as we move upstream and achieves grandeur as Kilnsey Crag comes into view. This great cliff has been cropped, smoothed and undercut by Wharfedale glaciers. Alice de Romille granted land at Kilnsey to Fountains Abbey in 1156 and a grange was developed as the focus for monastic farming in the area. Sheep were brought here in their hundreds for shearing, and the fleeces were then taken

away to the abbey in convoys of carts. Today Kilnsey is known for its show and for one of the most celebrated of fell races, when the runners ascend the steep flanks of the crag.

Just upstream of Kilnsey, Wharfedale is joined by a tributary dale of exceptional charm. The river is the Skirfare but the dale was once Amerdale and is now Littondale, taking its name from a hamlet lying well up the valley. The main village of this unspoilt dale is Arncliffe, a place as lovely as its setting. This was another grange of Fountains, granted to the abbey by Richard de Percy. When the village developed it took the form of farmsteads ranged around a large rectangular green; village England can offer no prettier picture than Arncliffe in June when the green becomes a shimmering golden sea of buttercups. The church was a Norman foundation and its parish extended into the wilds of upper Wharfedale. It experienced rebuildings in 1796 and 1841 but the sixteenth-century tower survived the changes. The Revd Charles Kingsley was a guest in Bridge End, an old house by the bridge in Arncliffe, and Littondale was the model for Vendale in his book *The Water Babies*. The Skirfare can be quite a torrent or may virtually disappear from sight, depending on the hydrological conditions in the underlying limestone. This is not a blind dale and via a long and right-angled route which passes between Fountains Fell, Plover Hill and Pen-y-ghent one eventually arrives in Ribblesdale at Stainforth.

Moving once more up the main valley of the Wharfe, the next village encountered is Kettlewell. In monastic times both the abbeys of Coverham and Fountains had territory here and Bolton Priory had estates close by. Because the servants of different orders lived cheek by jowl – cheek by cowl, if you prefer – the church was served by two priests. This was a remarkable arrangement everywhere but in Wharfedale, where Linton and Burnsall also had pairs of parsons. The first church was erected in the twelfth century, but the surviving one dates from 1820. Kettlewell is well served by footpaths and is a fine base for rambling. Drivers who are confident of the cooling systems in their engines can make the steep Park Rash ascent into Coverdale, part of an old coaching route from London to Richmond which passes through the fifteenth-century hunting reserve of the earls of Westmorland. Just below the watershed runs the bank and ditch of the Ta (or Tor) Dyke, an undated but almost certainly prehistoric frontier-work plainly built with great effort to keep the Wharfedale folk out of Wensleydale territory.

In the main valley Starbotton lies between the villages of Kettlewell and Buckden. It bears tribute to the fearsome power of floods in Wharfedale, the entire settlement being rebuilt after its destruction by the swollen Cam Gill Beck in 1686, when Kettlewell was also severely damaged by the Wharfe. This is one of several settlements in the Dales with close association with the Quakers. Several of the villages in Wharfedale have their roots in old monastic granges but Buckden reflects that other great use of the early medieval countryside of the Dales – hunting. Above Buckden, Wharfedale becomes Langstrothdale and here the Percy family created a great chase with ten hunting lodges. Buckden was occupied by the Percy foresters and even its name refers to the deer. Looming over the village is the 2303-foot (702-m) bulk of Buckden Pike. This great fell intercepted the glacier flowing down Langstrothdale and diverted it into two branches, one moving into Bishopdale and one into Wharfedale. The ice gouged Bishopdale into a typical 'U'-shaped glacial trough yet the mass of Buckden Pike shielded the valley of the Walden Beck, so in this tributary valley of Wensleydale one can get an impression of the pre-glacial countryside of the Dales.

Langstrothdale is a remote and secretive place. It was even more so in Chaucer's time, for in his *Reeve's Tale* he placed it 'farre in the north can I not tell where'. The beautiful church at Hubberholme is in the Pennine Perpendicular style and a chapel of ease of Arncliffe parish church has stood here for seven centuries. Next comes Yockenthwaite, a hamlet standing where a hamlet may have stood since Viking or even prehistoric times, while upstream of the one-arched bridge a 'stone circle' – more probably the kerb stones of an ancient tomb – lie close to the riverside. By the time one prepares to leave Wharfedale near Beckermonds hamlet the countryside has lost its sparkle in favour of a bleakness which will surely deteriorate into drabness as the conifers hereabouts mature or, as many do, simply die. But from Yockenthwaite down to Bolton Bridge Wharfedale offers as fine a stretch of finely wrought and crisply coloured countryside as one could ever hope to see.

Although the main dales exist as great corridors, each trending roughly north-west to south-east, each a distinctive little world, the Craven district in the south of the region is rather different. It may well have survived as a Celtic Christian outpost during the early years of English domination, just like the more celebrated kingdom of Elmet, around Leeds. It contains dales like Ribblesdale and Malhamdale, which are less coherent than those previously explored, the great gateways of Skipton and Settle and, if one steps over the Lancashire border, the Forest of Bowland. Malhamdale is one of the smallest of dales but also one of the most heavily visited. It is the valley of the upper Aire, which drops from Malham Tarn, flows briefly through a lovely valley section and runs beside Skipton before heading for the industrial landscapes of Airedale. Near Gargrave the Aire occupies a gap used as a pass across the Pennines since the days of the first traveller and exploited by road, rail and the Leeds–Liverpool Canal. Approaching the Dales from the busy A65 and Gargrave, the river is reached at Airton, an attractive village with a squatter's house of the seventeenth century standing on the green. This is another village with powerful Quaker associations. The Friends' Meeting House of 1700 was built by the linen-weaver William Ellis, who preached in North America before settling at Airton. Opposite is a house with 'WAE' carved on the doorhead to commemorate William and Alice, his wife. This was a village of linen-workers, the old mill by the river being built in the eighteenth century, rebuilt in 1838 and converted into flats in modern times. In so far as one can rely upon the translation of place-names, the nearby settlements of Scosthrop and Calton are the hamlets of Scottish Vikings and slaves respectively. Calton was the home of 'Honest' John Lambert, a friend of Oliver Cromwell who captured Bradford for the Parliamentarians and was exiled to Guernsey by Charles II (scant punishment for anyone but a dalesman).

Kirkby Malham is noted for its superb church in the Pennine Perpendicular style of the fifteenth and sixteenth centuries, here little diminished by a restoration in 1879. Fountains Abbey and Bolton Priory had estates in the vicinity of the village and were the providers of the Perpendicular church. As with several other Dales villages, the important industrial chapter in the history of Kirkby Malham is partly hidden, but the rectory was formerly a cotton-spinning mill and there was a bobbin mill beside the stream.

With the scenic crescendos of Malham Cove and Gordale Scar on either side, Malham is a magnet for visitors, and the large and seemingly

A corner of Clapham

uninviting car park on the outskirts of the village offers the only realistic prospect of a parking place. In the thirteenth century Malham passed into monastic control and existed as two manors, Malham West, which was a possession of Fountains Abbey and was centred on Malham Hall, and the Bolton Priory estates centred on Prior's Hall. Meanwhile at Bordley, close to the track to Kilnsey Grange, the monks of Fountains had a renowned horse-breeding station. After the dissolution of the monasteries the lands around Malham passed from large landowners and speculators to small freeholders in a pattern repeated in scores of Dales villages. During the 1790s zinc ore or calamine, which is combined with copper to make brass, was discovered near Malham and for a couple of decades the calamine mines supported industrial growth in the village. At the same time Malham fair had developed as a great venue for Scottish drovers of sheep and cattle. Gradually the long-distance trade declined and was overtaken by a more localised sheep fair. Malham Cove and Gordale Scar lie within walking distance of the village; if forced to choose between them I would always favour the brooding gorge of Gordale. Visitors to Gordale should explore the beck on the other side of the road and discover Janet's Foss. This lovely

waterfall is named after the queen of the local fairies, and sheep were *Scaleber Force*
washed in the pool at the foot of the falls.

At a height of 1229 feet (374 m) Malham Tarn is the loftiest lake in the
Pennines and it can be reached from Malham village by the more vigorous
of ramblers, many of whom will encounter other walkers plodding the
250-mile (400-km) Pennine Way from Edale in Derbyshire to Kirk Yetholm
in Scotland. Faulting has thrust impervious slates to the surface here while
glaciers dumped a barrier of gravel and clay across the existing stream. In
this way nature has created a watertight lake floor and a natural dam.
Gradually the lake is shrinking and at its western end the peat deposits
contain fragments of the pine and oak forest which cloaked the fells in
early-prehistoric times. Perhaps it was spawn clinging to legs of prehistoric
birds that introduced fish to the tarn and in the twelfth century William de
Percy granted the trout fishery to Fountains Abbey. Now Malham Tarn
House is a base for field studies in natural history and conservation.

Malham Tarn is noted for its trout, while further west the Ribble is a
salmon river. Near the headwaters of the Ribble, and close to the junction
of the B6255 and B6479, stands the famous Ribblehead Viaduct on the

Settle–Carlisle railway. This was the line that nobody wanted and British Rail tried to kill. It was opened in 1876 by the Midland Railway, the company being desperate to control its own route to Scotland as rivals owned the more practical coastal routes. The viaduct has twenty-four lofty arches built from enormous blocks of locally quarried limestone and standing on footings sunk deep through the sodden peat of Batty Moss. In the churchyard at Little Chapel-le-Dale to the south-west lie the bodies of 200 unnamed railway builders, most of whom died when smallpox erupted in the trackside shanty towns. In 1982 British Rail sought to kill the line by running down services and it seemed certain that the line would be lost owing to the viaduct's deterioration; driving rain has caused the decay of mortar and frost has cracked the stones. However, the proponents of closure failed to appreciate the powerful support mustered by a coalition of local rail-users, lovers of the Dales and railway enthusiasts, and there were 22,000 objections to the original closure proposal.

The setting of the Ribblehead viaduct is as bleak as any in the Pennines and so windswept that in 1964 a number of cars were blown off a passing train. By the time one has moved downstream as far as Horton-in-Ribblesdale the scenery has mellowed. Horton is a favourite base for the more energetic ramblers who tackle the three great surrounding peaks of Whernside, 2414 feet (736 m), Ingleborough, 2373 feet (723 m), and Pen-y-ghent, 2273 feet (693 m). Pen-y-ghent provides a wonderful back-drop to Horton's lovely and partly Norman church of St Oswald's. Much of the land here was owned by Jervaulx Abbey. Horton is ringed by peaks and by famous potholes like Alum Pot, Hull Pot and Pen-y-ghent Hole, while Stainforth, 3 miles (5 km) downstream, is bracketed by waterfalls, Stainforth Force to the west and Catrigg Force to the east. From the village one can follow an old pack-horse road over Pen-y-ghent Fell to Halton Gill at the head of Littondale or continue southwards through the former leather-tanning village of Langcliffe to Settle.

At Settle one encounters the busy A65, the main link between lowland Yorkshire and the Lake District. Two much visited villages lie in no important dale but close to the busy routeway. With its bridges, stone dwellings and fourteenth-century century church tower Clapham is one of the prettiest of Dales villages. It is the home of the celebrated magazine *The Dalesman* and Ingleborough Hall was the base from which the explorer and plant-collector Reginald Farrer (1880–1920) would set off for his adventures in the Far East. A lovely footpath leads past Ingleborough Cave and upwards to the vast maw of Gaping Gill Hole, where a winch and bosun's chair may be erected at Bank Holiday weekends. Ingleton, on the margins of Yorkshire and of the park, is less pretty than Clapham but a great centre for exploring numerous geological attractions. The church of St Mary has had a lively history; the original church was Norman but, with the exception of the thirteenth-century tower, the building seen today dates from 1887. In Commonwealth times the Norman font was cast into the Doe Beck but it was discovered and reinstated. The falls walk can be followed for 4 miles (6.4 km) via a ravine and a series of impressive falls, including the Pecca Falls, up to the great cascade of Thornton Force. A couple of miles along the road to Hawes are the White Scar Caves, an illuminated cavern system lying beneath the bulk of Ingleborough, while just across the River Doe are the Snow Falls.

Returning to Ribblesdale, lovers of great falls should travel a mile or so east of Settle on the little Kirkby Malham road to see the seldom visited Scaleber Force, where the white water plunges into a narrow wooded ravine. The falls lie on the Elgar Way. This, a circular route of 13 miles (21 km) through limestone country around Settle, was created by the popular Dales journalist and historian W. R. Mitchell, the recent discoverer of lost Elgar manuscripts. Elgar was a frequent guest of the local doctor, Charles William Buck, at Settle, where he composed 'Rosemary' and completed 'Salut d'Amour'.

Dales country continues south of Settle where the Ribble enters Lancashire's Forest of Bowland. This area was divided between several great abbeys. Kirkstall Abbey, near Leeds, had horse and cattle farms in the Slaidburn area and took hay from the meadows at Hammerton. Sawley Abbey was a daughter house of Fountains, founded by an abbot, twelve monks and ten lay brethren in 1147. The last Abbot of Sawley was a leader of the northern revolt, the Pilgrimage of Grace, and paid with his life for his support of the monastic cause which found such favour in the north. The Abbot of Whalley Abbey, which lies a little way downstream on the Ribble, met a similar fate. Whalley Abbey was a Cistercian foundation of 1296. Soon the monks of the two houses by the Ribble were in dispute over salmon-fishing rights. Meanwhile the area was designated, though scarcely used, as a royal hunting forest. After the dissolution of the monasteries there was some small-scale industrial activity. Silver ore was worked in the Slaidburn area in the seventeenth century. William Pudsay of Bolton Hall started a mint and coined his own shillings, reputedly escaping with a bold leap across the river bluff when the forgery was discovered.

When approached from Skipton or Settle the Ribblesdale section of the Forest of Bowland can be reached via Gisburn or the A59. Gisburn Park was the home of the first Lord Ribblesdale (1752–1826), a pioneer conservationist who planted 1,200,000 oaks and other trees beside the Ribble. He also tried, in vain, to buy up the land which would enable him to ride from Pendle Hill to Malham without leaving his own property.

One of the prettiest villages in all the Dales lies about 3 miles (5 km) to the west by a tributary of the Ribble. Bolton-by-Bowland along with Gisburn was among the one hundred Yorkshire manors granted to William de Percy in 1067. By 1190 a church was built at Bolton and in the reign of Edward III the village was granted a fair. As a fugitive, Henry VI (1422–61 and 1470–1) was sheltered by Ralph de Pudsay at Bolton Hall and it is claimed that this humble, pacifist King designed the church tower at Bolton-by-Bowland. It is ornate in the manner of a west-country tower rather than belonging to the more austere northern tradition. The earliest masonry here belongs to the thirteenth century but the church is largely the result of rebuilding by Sir Ralph de Pudsay around 1466–7. Perhaps the King did exert an influence on the design of the church prior to his recapture in 1465. He was seized by members of the Yorkist Talbot family when crossing the Ribble on stepping stones at Brungerley. In the graveyard of Bolton-by-Bowland church is the tomb of Sir Ralph, who died in 1468; it depicts his three (successive) wives and his twenty-five children. In the seventeenth and eighteenth centuries status in the community was reflected by the place where one sat or stood in church, and worshippers were very territorial. Here the pews of 1694 are carved with the initials of their occupants.

One village which can rival Bolton's claim to be the prettiest in Lancashire is Downham, to the west of the Ribble and a couple of miles south of Sawley. It lies in the shadow of Pendle Hill, associated with the Pendle Witches who were tried in 1612. Two of the families involved, the Chattox and Demdike clans, had evil reputations, but Alice Nutter of Roughlee may have allowed the accusations against herself to stand rather than betray her true loyalties to the persecuted Catholic cause.

CHAPTER 18

The Future of the Dales

More by accident than design, the Yorkshire Dales have endured to the 1990s as an area where unspoiled and little-spoiled countryside greatly exceeds the areas ruined by modern development. As the region has been so fortunate one might imagine that no effort would be spared to preserve it. In fact its forthcoming ruination is now widely expected and the debate seems mainly to concern the form that it will take.

As the relatively recent fate of Nidderdale (lying outside the National Park) reveals, the desecration of the other dales would probably be well advanced by now were it not for the existence of the Yorkshire Dales National Park. This is one of ten such parks created under the National Parks and Access to the Countryside Act of 1949, but its value was instantly diminished by the provision of boundaries which excluded great tracts of excellent Dales countryside in Nidderdale, lower Wensleydale and Ribblesdale. The National Park Committee is a component of the county council and has the powers of a planning authority but only modest means to influence the behaviour of visitors and landowners. Perhaps the most glaring weakness is reflected in its inability to stem the destruction of entire landmarks by the quarrying interests. A professional staff of about fifty is employed but their expert advice has to be filtered through the system of local democracy and vested interests, so that what emerges in the form of decisions and policy may be of diminished value.

Despite its blissful aspects, the Dales countryside is fraught with tensions and conflicting interests. Land does not have to be of high quality and value to attract competing interests and poor hill land may be competed for by farming, forestry, quarrying or shooting concerns. While the National Park authorities seek to harmonise these different forms of land use the search for consensus is hamstrung by the fact that several activities are simply incompatible. The expansion of commercial forestry is difficult to justify on pure economic grounds and is impossible to reconcile with any attempt to conserve the countryside. Power-boats and trail-bikes destroy the tranquillity which most ramblers seek, while canoeing imposes intolerable stresses on riverside wildlife and anglers too. Among Dalesfolk the most unpopular activity of all is the use of the area for low-level flying by NATO aircraft – one cannot help believing that were SAM missiles for sale in the post offices at Pateley Bridge and Grassington then RAF Fighter Command would soon cease to exist. I suspect people in the Dales would happily stand exposed to the threat of invasion by Lithuania or Turkmenistan in exchange for the removal of the terror from the Tornado and Phantom jets, which is accentuated by the fast and low approaches giving little or no warning of the thunder about to erupt. Visitors knocked almost senseless by the passage of one aircraft should instantly prepare for the next assault on their sanity, for the planes travel in twos and threes.

In terms of the village landscapes the great threat concerns the pressure for new housing development. Thousands and thousands of people would like to live in the Dales, and if they all did then of course the whole character of the region would be undermined and its attractions would vanish. Currently developers smile from the sidelines as muddle-headed and more cynical interests build up the pressure for expansion in each village. Questionnaires are circulated to produce the 'facts' needed to support the case. In one village, for example, the surveys at the time of writing showed that most people preferred that things should remain as they are, but a minority of people would like to have new houses in the village – at prices of £20,000–£30,000. At this time in the same village a tiny single-storey outbuilding, hitherto considered uninhabitable, was sold for £65,000, and no new house, however mean, could be bought for less. The housing problem since the mid-1980s has been caused by the phenomenal rise in prices, itself partly caused by an influx of rich southerners. In the past, indigenous housing needs could be met by the building of council houses, but since tenants have been able to buy their dwellings councils have been understandably reluctant to build new ones. On one Dales village estate, for example, a long-term tenant can buy his house with a market value of £80,000 for just £17,000 from the council. In the 'highly desirable' village of Grassington some council houses are now holiday homes while young folk born and bred in the village move out to Skipton in search of affordable dwellings.

Were employment in the Dales growing then the need for new houses would be hard to refute but it is not. The decline of traditional textile industries and lead-mining followed by the mechanisation and 'rationalisation' of farming caused population levels to plummet. Muker parish in Swaledale had a population of 1119 in 1801 and one of 322 in 1971. For East Witton Without in Wensleydale the figures are 294 and 62, for Dent,

1773 and 590 and for Malham 262 and 163. Apart from the modest seasonal work deriving from the tourist industry there is no significant growth in local employment, so any new houses built will be occupied either by commuters or by retired people, mainly from outside the region.

It is hard to see how even the best planning policies could recreate the region's finest asset – its people. On the family farms new generations of Dalesfolk will be created so long as the hill farmers can stay in business. Elsewhere, however, it is plain that as the old villagers die a new community of 'off-comers' or 'off-cumdens' expands and the qualities of the hard-shelled but soft-centred Dales character are lost. Though Dalesfolk and Scots were once the fiercest of foes, both have much in common and are developing similar attitudes to what are often regarded as the plastic people from the south. When at school in a Dales village in the 1950s I remember that all of us spoke the Dales dialect, though some more strongly than others. Now one could spend a week in the village without hearing that wonderful accent.

In 1989 the renowned investigator of the politics of the environment, Professor Timothy O'Riordan, joined forces with Dr Christopher Wood of the National Park, researcher Ann Shadrake and artist Hannah Chester-man to develop various scenarios of how the landscape of the Dales may develop. The wilderness scenario concerned the impact of 'set-aside' policies to reduce EEC agricultural production. With rich southern farmers switching from arable to livestock, much land in the Dales might revert to wilderness. This would benefit wildlife but would result in the decay of hill-farming life and force surviving farmers to develop their facilities for attracting ramblers.

The reverse scenario is one in which further incentives are given to farmers without consideration for conservation. More ugly farm buildings are erected, woods are felled, walls and hedgerows removed, field barns abandoned and the remaining herb- and flower-rich meadows disappear. A far more attractive countryside is retained in a scenario where farmers are given an environmental subsidy which rewards them for preserving the wildlife habitats rather than for boosting their production. At present the Environmentally Sensitive Area subsidies are only available in 6 per cent of the area of the Dales but the expansion of the scheme would be very costly, though welcome.

A ghastly scenario results from the encouragement of hunting–shooting–fishing interests. Although the grouse moors are maintained and some new woods are planted as game cover the old hill sheep-farming tradition is allowed to decay, along with those barns which are not converted into luxury accommodation for the bloodsports enthusiasts. The world of the Victorian estate owner is recreated with the common throng reduced to employment as beaters and skivvies.

In *The Dalesman* in 1989, Colin Speakman, a leading conservationist in the area, wrote:

> We must be under no illusion. Over the next few years the Yorkshire Dales are going to be under considerable pressure from outside interests to become a kind of playground of a newly affluent society with little or no respect or understanding of the traditional culture and way of life of the area.

Visually, the world described by James Herriot has survived almost intact, but it is like a fragile shell which conceals a ferment of tensions and pressures for change of the most destructive kind. Sadly lacking during this period of change has been any coherent national view of what the region should be and of how policies could be harmonised to achieve this condition. Most readers, one presumes, would prefer the countrysides to remain much as they are. Yet this can only be achieved by a wholehearted policy of perpetuating the small farm and of subsidising the small farmer to conserve the traditional features of the landscape. Such interventionist policies conflict with the entire thrust of government values during the 1980s, a decade in which a view of the horrors in store for the Yorkshire Dales was revealed to the local communities.

One conclusion is inescapable: the small farmer made the Yorkshire Dales and, when he goes, so too do the priceless vistas of meadow, pasture, wall and barn. In a strange way it is not poverty which threatens the region – the Dalesfolk have coped with poverty for centuries – but wealth. The enchanting beauty wrought over the centuries by the poor people of the Dales may be defaced by rich outsiders in the space of just a few decades.

Those who are deeply concerned for the future of this unique region may find encouragement through membership of the Yorkshire Dales Society. The address is 153 Main Street, Addingham, Ilkley, LS29 0LY.

Bibliography

Bogg, Edmund, *From Edenvale to the Plains of York*, Edmund Bogg, c. 1900.

Brooks, Susan D., *A History of Grassington*, Dalesman Books, 1979.

Grainge, William, *The History and Topography of Harrogate and the Forest of Knaresborough*, John Russell Smith, 1871.

Harker, Ronald (ed.), *Timble Man: Diaries of a Dalesman*, Hendon, 1988.

Hartley, Marie and Ingilby, Joan, *The Yorkshire Dales*, J. M. Dent, 1963.

——*Life and Tradition in the Yorkshire Dales*, J. M. Dent, 1968.

Home, Gordon, *Yorkshire Dales and Fells*, A. C. Black, 1906.

Illingworth, J. L., *Yorkshire's Ruined Castles*, ed. J. Burrow, S. R. Publishers, 1938.

Jennings, Bernard (ed.), *A History of Nidderdale*, Advertiser Press, 1967.

Lee, Brian (ed.), *Lead Mining in Swaledale*, Faust, 1985.

Lucas, Joseph, *Studies in Nidderdale*, Elliot Stock, c. 1875.

Mitchell, W. R., *The Changing Dales*, Dalesman Books, 1980.

Raistrick, Arthur, *The Pennine Dales*, Eyre Methuen, 1968.

——*Green Roads in the Mid Pennines*, Moorland, 1974.

——*Monks and Shepherds in the Yorkshire Dales*, Yorkshire Dales National Park Committee, 1980.

——*Buildings in the Yorkshire Dales*, Dalesman Books, 1981.

——*Malham and Malham Moor*, Dalesman Books, 1983.

Sampson, John, *From Edenvale to the Plains of York*, 1900.

——*Higher Wharfedale*, Dalesman Books, 1904.

Speight, Harry, *Nidderdale*, Elliot Stock, 1906.

Waltham, Tony, *Caves, Crags and Gorges*, Constable, 1984.

——*Yorkshire Dales National Park*, Webb & Bower, 1987.

Women's Institute of Burnt Yates, *The Township of Clint cum Hamlets*, Burnt Yates WI, 1982.

Wright, Geoffrey N., *Roads and Trackways of the Yorkshire Dales*, Moorland, 1985.

Index